Praise for

A THOUSAND TINY PAPER CUTS

"[Spearing] is eloquent and precise in her critiques of high-control Christianity. . . . Believers who've been harmed by church communities will find strength and understanding."
—PUBLISHERS WEEKLY

"From the spiritual abuse glossary (a healing resource in and of itself!) to Katherine's story and professional take on spiritual abuse, *A Thousand Tiny Paper Cuts* pulled me in right from the beginning!! For anyone trying to make sense of their journey through the confusing maze of religious abuse recovery, Katherine's treatment of this topic is authentic, courageous, original, clear, humorous and deeply true—a roadmap for any and all on their journey towards healing."
—CONNIE A. BAKER, MA, LPC

"For everyone who's ever taken a chance—or wanted to take a chance—on escaping the constraints of high-control religion, *A Thousand Tiny Paper Cuts* will validate and fortify you. Filled with insights on how God-talk is often used to enforce conformity and coerce compliance, this book provides manna for the journey toward a life unbounded."
—CHRISTA BROWN, AUTHOR OF *BAPTISTLAND*

"*A Thousand Tiny Paper Cuts* lays bare the thin, often invisible line between growing up in a cult and simply being raised 'a devout Christian' in America. It makes a powerful case that the real work of healing doesn't end just because you leave the system. It's a grueling, ongoing struggle of grieving that begins where the escape story ends." —MATTIE JO COWSERT, AUTHOR OF *GOD, SEX, AND RICH PEOPLE*

"Katherine Spearing's *A Thousand Tiny Paper Cuts* is a vital, personal guide for survivors of spiritual abuse. With practical wisdom, it illuminates the path to healing and empowerment, offering hope and humor for those reclaiming their lives from coercive control." —SARAH EDMONDSON, AUTHOR OF *SCARRED: THE TRUE STORY OF HOW I ESCAPED NXIVM, THE CULT THAT BOUND MY LIFE* AND HOST *A LITTLE BIT CULTY PODCAST*

"With haunting prose, Spearing tells of the ways that spiritual abuse continues to find many of us in the dark. Even more remarkably, she captures how longing can sit alongside terror, how dreams can grow stubbornly against our fears. For all its probing of white evangelicalism's dark heart, this is a soulful book." —AUDREY CLARE FARLEY, AUTHOR OF *GIRLS AND THEIR MONSTERS*

"With her years of experience working with and advocating for survivors, Katherine Spearing is an important voice on the issue of spiritual abuse in the American evangelical church. She shares her deep, hard-earned insight into the insidiousness and complexity of this form of abuse and how to heal from religious trauma. This book is an incredibly valuable resource for survivors and for those who love them."

—CAIT WEST, AUTHOR OF

RIFT: A MEMOIR OF BREAKING AWAY FROM CHRISTIAN PATRIARCHY

"In *A Thousand Tiny Paper Cuts,* Katherine Spearing speaks with an unabashed vulnerability that will resonate with those breaking free from toxic religious patriarchy. Her story and wisdom effectively portray how spiritual abuse can occur with or without physical harm. Spearing leaves no stone unturned as she provides grace and hope to all who are healing."

—JANYNE MCCONNAUGHEY, PHD,

AUTHOR OF *TRAUMA IN THE PEWS,*

CO-FOUNDER OF RELIGIOUS TRAUMA NETWORK

"Katherine Spearing so eloquently shows how high demand religion is the perfect enabler for abuse by enforcing strict gender roles, forbidding questioning authority, and enforcing the patriarchy. Read this book if you too have taken the courageous and completely life altering path of faith deconstruction, leaving high demand religion, or even just a conservative upbringing."

—LUCY ROWETT, CSC.

CERTIFIED SEX COACH AND SEXOLOGIST

"It's imperative that spiritual abuse survivors have a common vocabulary that describes what happened to them, as well as the manipulation tactics used by those with power. The lexicon that Katherine Spearing offers is an important first step for healing, as well as the start to reimagining what life-giving spirituality and relationships could look like."

—JEREMIAH GIBSON AND JULIA POSTEMA,

HOSTS OF THE *SEXVANGELICALS PODCAST*

"Katherine Spearing is an impressive presence in this field. Because of her experiences and insights, she has the unique ability to understand that it is because of a succession of countless harmful events and teachings that one is left needing care and healing in order to feel capable in this world and hopeful about the future." —RACHEL BERNSTEIN LMFT, HOST OF *INDOCTRINATION PODCAST*

A Thousand Tiny Paper Cuts is a no-holds-barred guide for individuals seeking a fulfilling life beyond spiritual abuse and religious trauma. Author Katherine Spearing blends lived experience, professional insight, and fierce advocacy for the life that matters most: her own. She's a bold model for anyone who dares to be whole after being diminished by patriarchy." —GERETTE BUGLION, AUTHOR OF *AN EVERYDAY CULT*

A Thousand Tiny Paper Cuts is a piercing, necessary exploration of spiritual abuse that validates the quiet pain so many carry. Katherine Spearing writes with clarity, compassion, intellect and strength—offering not just understanding, but hope." —KRISTINA HART, WRITER, COMEDIAN, ADVOCATE

A
THOUSAND
TINY
PAPER
CUTS

A THOUSAND TINY PAPER CUTS

The Subtle, Insidious Nature of Spiritual Abuse
and Life on the Other Side

KATHERINE SPEARING
Founder of Tears of Eden

LAKE
DRIVE
lakedrivebooks.com

Lake Drive Books
6757 Cascade Road SE, #162
Grand Rapids, MI 49546
info@lakedrivebooks.com

lakedrivebooks.com
@lakedrivebooks

Publishing books that help you heal, grow, and discover.

A Thousand Tiny Paper Cuts

Paperback ISBN: 978-1-957687-62-9
E-book ISBN: 978-1-957687-63-6

Library of Congress Control Number: 2025900180

Cover and interior design by Laura Duffy
Author photo by Joy McCullough

Details of most locations have been obscured and names of people have been changed to protect privacy except pertaining to public figures or where permission was obtained. Most conversations are recounted how the author remembers them, and situations are written from the author's perspective, encompassing the author's opinion.

While the content addresses trauma and the dynamics of abuse, it is not a substitute for individualized care. The reader is encouraged to consult a mental health or medical professional before adopting any principles or suggestions offered in this book.

For more resources on spiritual abuse, see www.tearsofeden.org.

To work with a mental health professional specializing in spiritual abuse recovery, consult www.traumaresolutionandrecovery.com.

DEDICATION

To every woman who didn't fit in the church,
Whose questions got you kicked out of Sunday school,
Whose power got you labeled bitch and Jezebel,
Whose ambition terrified the power hoarders,

Who stopped waiting for a seat at the table and built your own table.

CONTENTS

FOREWORD

June 2, 2000. My best friend and I were leading the rest of our high school class out the doors of our gymnasium where our friends and family would shortly follow. Pictures, hugs, and lots of tears would commence, and congratulations would be offered because we had all just graduated. As my best friend and I burst through the doors, tasting our first moments of true adulthood, my head intuitively turned to the right—toward the highway. Going either direction on this highway led out to a life that was bigger than what this tiny town could offer.

I felt my heart pulling toward the highway. I knew life was bigger than what I had been allowed to imagine. But I was at a crossroads—an existential crisis of sorts. I had received acceptance, scholarships, and financial aid packages from every college I applied to; I wanted to go. But no matter how excited I was or how many conversations I had, my parents simply were not going to let me go away. Instead, I was allowed to go to the local community college and live at home, waiting for my future husband to appear so we could get married and begin our own family.

The knowledge that life was bigger and that there was more "out there" never left. But I had to suppress the hope that it built in me as I was told by all of the influences around me that my highest calling was not to do, or go, or be. Instead, it was to stay, to submit, to bear. At seventeen years old, I didn't have the resources or mental fortitude to put up a fight, so I complied.

The hope, though, never went away. Eventually it motivated me to get my bachelor's degree and then my master's. It motivated me to leave my community and start life on my own ten years after I longingly looked at the highway on the night of my high school graduation. That hope became the quiet engine of my healing—a journey that meant recognizing the traumatic impacts of high-control religion, patriarchy, and relational dynamics rooted in power and control. A journey that eventually taught me that healing is a living practice rather than a destination where we arrive.

———————————

As a psychotherapist and trauma coach, sometimes my clients will ask me if I have magical powers. I usually chuckle, but I know what they mean. They are wondering how it is that I can predict, with accuracy, the next moves of the individual or group that is perpetrating harm against them. They are stunned when I invite them to be on the lookout for specific behavior, language, or relational patterns that may occur—only to witness those very things firsthand in their life between sessions.

Abuse and dynamics of power and control are a lot of things. They are harmful and insidious. They create long lasting impacts. They make you feel crazy. One thing they are not? Creative.

Unsurprisingly, I don't have magical powers. However, I do have over two decades of experiences in professional, clinical, and academic settings and even more in personal experiences that have taught me exactly how dynamics of power and control work. Regardless of whether the perpetrator is an individual, a group, or an entire system, the playbook is the same. They abide by specific patterns and habits, which are easy to track when you know what you're looking for.

However, until the last decade or so, this pattern recognition has not been focused on religion. Culturally speaking, religion is often an untouchable institution. It's personal, sacred, and often the basis for one's identity. Examining it, let alone critiquing it, has not been taken too kindly. And yet, that is exactly the problem. When harm hides behind holiness, it becomes even harder to name—and even harder to leave.

Dynamics of power and control within religion are virtually the same as dynamics within relationships (such as domestically violent relationships). But within religion, there is an added component: God. When the abuse and control is sanctioned by God and the people he has put in authority, to question it or push back often equates to sin. And with sin comes spiritual consequences.

What makes religious abuse so dangerous is not just the patterns themselves—it's how effectively they hide in plain sight.

When a partner isolates you, controls your access to resources, shames your feelings, and demands obedience, we call it abuse. But when a pastor does it? We're told it's discipleship. When a parent enforces silence and submission using scripture, we call it righteousness. When an institution strips you of your agency, your voice, your body, and tells you it's God's will, we are conditioned to praise it as holy sacrifice.

The truth is, spiritual abuse often looks like faithfulness on the outside and feels like death on the inside. It's a slow bleed. A thousand tiny paper cuts, each justified with a verse, a prayer, or a smile, until one day, you wake up and realize you've been hemorrhaging for years.

That's what Katherine captures in these pages.

As I read, I found myself nodding, wincing, tearing up—because these are not just her stories. They are ours. They are mine. So many of the same scenes, the same silences, the same shame showed up in my own life. I recognized the gas-lighting cloaked as concern, the coercion baptized in Scripture, the hollow applause for obedience that cost me my voice, my dreams, my body.

Katherine gives language to the invisible wounds and fractured identities left behind by high-control religion. And she does so with a rare mix of wit, honesty, and tenderness. This book is not simply a memoir. It is a mirror, a map, and a companion.

Healing from this kind of abuse requires more than logic or theology. It requires grief. It requires community. It requires body-based healing, spiritual reclamation, and deep permission to rage, to rest, to imagine a life outside of control. It asks us to deconstruct not only what we were taught, but how we learned to survive inside it.

Because the impact of spiritual abuse is multidimensional, our healing must be too.

This book will not give you neat answers. But it will give you language. It will give you resonance. It will give you back parts of yourself you didn't realize were stolen.

Whether you are just beginning to name the harm or are years into your healing, may this book serve as a companion. May it remind you that you are not alone. And may it point you back to the sacred truth that your story, your body, your voice, and your freedom were never the problem.

They were what the system feared most, because they are the very things that will set you free.

–DR. LAURA ANDERSON, LMFT
PSYCHOTHERAPIST, AUTHOR, AND FOUNDER OF THE
CENTER FOR TRAUMA RESOLUTION AND RECOVERY

SPIRITUAL ABUSE GLOSSARY

benevolent sexism: When a man appears kind and thoughtful but his actions increase the inequality between genders. In patriarchal spaces, there's an emphasis on men protecting and taking care of women, but this often happens in a way that removes a woman's agency and increases the man's control. Benevolent sexism can be seen as control in the name of protection and care.

BITE model: Steven Hassan's model showing that cults control Behavior, Information, Thoughts, and Emotions.

Christian patriarchy: An ideology that espouses that God made men the head of the family and the church and that God made women to serve men and raise children.

clergy sexual abuse: Sexual activity between a clergy person and a member of their congregation (adult or child) who is not their spouse. Includes physical and nonphysical interactions.

complementarianism: Theological belief in the equality of the sexes, but equality with different roles. Men are supposed to be the spiritual leaders of the home, and only men can be elders and pastors in the church. See also **egalitarianism.**

DARVO: From Jennifer J. Freyd, PhD. Stands for Deny, Attack, and Reverse Victim and Offender. The perpetrator or offender may Deny the behavior, Attack the individual who is confronting them, and then Reverse the roles of Victim and Offender, which happens when the perpetrator assumes the role of victim and turns the true victim—or the whistleblower—into an alleged offender.

egalitarianism: Theological belief in the equality of genders. No profession or role is off limits to someone based on their gender. See also "Complementarianism."

financial abuse: Using finances to manipulate, coerce, control, and exploit. Common examples include regulating someone's access to employment, creating arbitrary debts, withholding money rightly owed, reneging on a financial agreement, and withholding money or possessions as punishment.

gaslighting: A manipulative tactic where an abuser sets out to make their victim question their sense of reality. If they can discredit the victim by appearing calm in the face of their victim's emotional appeals, then most people will side with the abuser and write the victim off as unstable.

Jezebel/Jezebel spirit: A sexist insult usually aimed at women who do not fall into prescribed Christian feminine ideals.

phobia (post high-control environment): An extreme bout of fear after leaving a high-control environment. In the context of spiritual abuse, it is often described as a fear of God striking you down by lightning. It can present as panic, heart palpitations, sleeplessness, and convulsions. Typically, your mind begins drawing up horrible possible catastrophes that might befall you—the worst of which is that God has rejected you and you will never again return to God's good graces.

purity culture: Religiously sanctioned regulation of sex, sexuality, and bodies. Common examples include shaming women for wearing clothing the culture deems immodest, shaming individuals for thoughts the culture deems impure, and punishing individuals for engaging in sexual activity outside of marriage between one man and one woman.

religious trauma: The impact of adverse religious experiences, resulting in trauma in the body. May be a result of abuse or the result of internalizing a harmful doctrine or harmful experience within a religious community.

somatic healing: A therapeutic modality of working with the body to access the trauma our cognitive minds can't reach. A foundation of this modality is the belief that our bodies are good and that the sensations in our bodies provide valuable information for healing.

spiritual abuse: Abuse that occurs within a religious context, including the deliberate use of God and a sacred text to manipulate, coerce, control, and exploit.

spiritual bypassing: Using God or scripture to avoid pain or grief, either our own or the pain of another. Can become abusive if someone is shamed for their expression of pain or grief.

stay-at-home daughter: A woman who is required by a specific Christian teaching to stay under her father's authority (often required to remain in his physical home) until she is married to a man.

survival response: A physical reaction, often involuntary, to an unsafe situation, real or perceived. Commonly known as fight, flight, or freeze. See also **trauma response.**

toxic positivity: Positivity at all costs, even in the face of grief, trauma, and abuse. Always finding the silver lining to the point of dishonesty about difficult circumstances.

trauma response: An involuntary bodily reaction to an experience that reminds the person of a time when they were unsafe. Indicates the nervous system has retained damage and is unable to determine that the body is safe in the present day. The individual must actually be safe in order to exhibit a trauma response; otherwise it is a survival response. See also **survival response.**

TO READ BEFORE READING

On April 10, 2024, I opened applications for a support group for survivors of spiritual abuse through the nonprofit I founded, Tears of Eden. I sent the announcement to the 189 people on our waitlist and monitored the application platform, refreshing my browser every few minutes, with the intention of capping the group at fifteen people.

In less than one hour, we had nineteen participants. This beat the record from the previous group, which filled up in three hours, which beat the group before it, which filled up in forty-eight hours. Survivors of spiritual abuse not only exist, they have an enormous need for education, care, and validation.

One reason such a need exists is due to the complex and covert nature of spiritual abuse. The stories are rarely a sonic boom or climactic explosion. You might not be aware of the abuse at all, which is one of the very reasons the impact can be so devastating—you don't know anything is wrong until long after the damage is done.

The absolute best description I've ever heard on the impact of spiritual abuse came from another survivor. They said, "It's like a thousand tiny paper cuts until eventually you bleed to death." A paper cut is frustrating and painful, but no one will rush you to urgent care over it. Nobody will bring you a casserole or write you a sympathy card.

One or two cuts might not be enough to cause alarm, but if you receive a thousand of these cuts over an extended period, eventually these minor cuts will consume your whole body. It's why when someone asks me, "What exactly is spiritual abuse?" I have to share a few stories, coupled with information about the impact of the abuse and all the work it takes to recover, to really explain it to someone who hasn't been there. Sometimes, you feel pressure to tell them the most sensational stories just to keep their attention.

This is why spiritual abuse is so complex. Most people want a brief example, something that will turn on the light in their prefrontal cortex, creating an aha moment: *That's spiritual abuse!* But a simple definition will not suffice if someone is unaware they've encountered it or if they've never been exposed to it. Typically, the only way to explain it is by telling a story, which often requires the storyteller to have a personal experience.

I try to explain it by first providing the simple definition they're often looking for: "Spiritual abuse is anything using God or the Bible to cause shame and harm, but it's much more complex than that." Then I tell them a story. I might tell the story from middle school years when my father chastised me for crying over a difficult math problem, telling me I wasn't trusting God. Shaming a child when they are struggling is emotional abuse. Using God to support that shame? That's spiritual abuse.

Or I might share a story from when I worked in professional ministry. I was once working for a church where I asked to speak with my boss in order to share how his lack of communication was causing confusion for me. He responded to my request for change with a deluge of barbs and darts. He berated me for two hours, attacking my character and accusing me of disrespect and trying to steal his job. (None of these things were true.) This was emotional, verbal, and psychological abuse. But because we worked for a church—a religious context—and because he used God to back his authority, this was also spiritual abuse.

Some in the spiritual abuse recovery world debate if spiritual abuse is a unique form of abuse or an umbrella term for other abuses. It is my opinion that it's both, but you rarely have spiritual abuse all on its own. Just like you rarely have physical abuse without emotional abuse or sexual abuse without psychological abuse, other forms of abuse are typically mixed in with it.

Which brings us to a discussion of the definition of abuse. You'll find many versions on the internet and in texts. I will define abuse as one person or system using their power to take away the agency of another person (or group of people) for self-serving purposes (such as self-gratification, control, financial gain, etc.).

This is where spiritual abuse gets tricky. While many abusers intentionally seek their own gratification by violating another, there are even more people spiritually abusing others while truly believing they are doing the will of God and acting in the best interests of the ones they abuse. You'll stare into the eyes of someone who you believe is a genuinely good human being, who you love and respect, as they attack your soul and damn you to hell. Good people often abuse other good people in the name of God. These wounds often go far deeper than the ones we receive from people who explicitly want to hurt us.

A helpful lens through which we might view spiritual abuse in Christianity is the lens of family. The institutional church describes itself as family and often becomes a surrogate family or fills gaps left by a family of origin. The impact of spiritual abuse is not unlike domestic abuse, as the damage caused by an abusive spiritual figure is not unlike the damage caused by an abusive parent. Luckily (or perhaps unluckily), I have extensive experience with both.

In this book, I will share examples of spiritual abuse from high-control communities that identify as Christian, which will include examples from fundamentalist Christianity and mainstream evangelicalism. (However, I refrain from drawing attention to any specific denomination, as I believe this abuse is rampant in all of evangelicalism. No denomination is safe.) While I believe anyone who has experienced abuse inside another religious group will glean helpful insights into their experience, I will not explore other religions for the main reason that those religions are outside of my scope of competency. While I studied most major religions in graduate school, I am not a specialist on any religion other than Christianity.

Also, for the scope of this book, I will share many examples from my own life. One of the most validating moments for a survivor is the moment they sit across the table from someone, look them in the eyes, and hear them say, "Me too." This book is my "Me too" for survivors. Because this book is using my story as the primary example, I acknowledge the stories may not fully resonate with everyone, as I am limited by my experience and various identities, specifically my identity as an able-bodied white woman who can move through the world presenting as cisgender and straight.

Art is an important part of my healing journey and plays a role in recovery for many survivors. I'll take artistic interludes within chapters to capture the truth in a way that is less direct (but no less true). I hope these interludes will function as an emotional break from a heavy subject.

While I may quote scripture and how it was used to abuse, I will not spend a lot of time dissecting scripture or telling the reader what the verses may or may not actually mean. I will, however, show the psychological and social aspects that create a structure for spiritually abusive religion.

A reader might seek out a book on spiritual abuse looking for a clean-cut list of abusive behaviors, or a book or article with a title like "Five Characteristics of an Abusive Church" or "Four Signs You're Working with an Abusive Pastor." This story is not without signs and characteristics with the hope of providing clarity, but I intentionally avoid focusing too much on behavior, as one of the characteristics of an abuser is their ability to modify their behavior to suit the needs of their target community. This book is for the survivors and those who support them. It is not meant to teach an institution how to avoid abuse (or the appearance of it).

While I will be discussing abuse that occurs within a religious context, this is not a religious book. I do not have an expectation for where the reader lands on the religious spectrum. From my professional work with survivors (through Tears of Eden and as a mental health professional), I know many find hope and healing in continued faith of some kind. I know just as many survivors (possibly more) who do not. And then, there are all the folks in between (which is a lovely and legitimate place to explore).

Trauma impacts the physical body and can show up following situations where we felt powerless. For that reason, religion is only helpful if the survivor participates with authentic consent. But religious affiliation is not required to pursue healing. For many, taking an indefinite break from Christianity (or any religion) is an important step in their healing process.

Several years ago, when I was doing research on spiritual abuse and considering starting a nonprofit for survivors (which eventually became Tears of Eden), I encountered a husband and wife who ran a treatment center for folks who had survived cults. Many of these survivors came from Bible-based cults. Some came from gangs. Gangs use cultic methods of coercive control to keep people from leaving. I found the similarities fascinating.

The husband told me we encounter three types of people when we're telling our stories. One type will believe us immediately. A second will dismiss us immediately. A third type will eventually believe us; they just need a little explanation.

May this book provide language and examples to assist that explanation for the survivor who chooses to tell their story.

ONE: POWER

At the Center of Abuse

Every time I enter a crosswalk, I'm afraid I'm going to die. The largest hazard to walking in the city is something incredibly dangerous to pedestrians: cars.

I love walking around my city. I prefer concrete to grass and high-rises to trees. I love exploring new places on foot. But each time I go out for a long walk, I'm acutely aware of the potential danger, especially when I set foot in a crosswalk.

Pedestrians have a right to cross the street in a crosswalk. The law requires drivers stop their cars to let the walker pass. Even so, each time I enter a crosswalk, I attempt to make eye contact with the drivers to ensure they see me. All it takes is one driver not paying attention for me to be a goner.

No matter how many laws or consequences exist to protect the pedestrian in the crosswalk, a car with a driver will always be bigger. It will always be stronger. It will always have the power to kill a person, regardless of the intentions of the driver.

Power is a word that arises often in the abuse recovery world. Who has the power is a critical component to determine who is able to give authentic consent. It's vital for noticing where the abuse originates.

Just like moving cars will always be bigger and stronger than walking people, power differentials will always exist. In the evangelical church, power differentials not only exist, they're often protected by systems using God and the Bible to coerce and control. Some examples consist of systemically supported hierarchies among genders, sexual orientations, and marital statuses.

It's important that we are mindful of these power differentials, noticing when someone uses their power to take away the autonomy of someone else. Misuse of power is where abuse occurs. To understand abuse, we must locate the center of power. Who has it? How are they wielding it? Are they aware of the impact of their power?

For recovery, the survivor must recognize and access their personal power. Part of the recovery process includes noticing when and how our power was taken from us. Then we take steps to reclaim it. Perhaps we may even claim our power for the very first time.

Sometimes abuse survivors have to go back to the beginning, to the moment the abuser suggested they knew best or said their actions were for our good. We follow the threads, noticing the different patterns. Then, we tell the story with our own words. Slowly and cautiously at first, because we are not used to our words. We don't know the sound of our own voice. Maybe we did once, but it's been drowned out by the narrative of the abuser and the abusive system.

We tell our stories. Then, sentence by sentence, we take our power back.

HONOR THY FATHER

That Sunday would change my life forever.

Southern weather is unpredictable and rarely pleasant. You spend most summer days dashing from the indoor AC to the pool. The first few minutes in a sun-soaked car are the very definition of misery. I imagine it is what every day in hell might feel like.

On a rare pleasant day when I was sixteen, my father held family church outdoors. It was a gathering of just my parents, siblings, and me. (While we often participated in communal, organized religion, my father positioned himself as my primary spiritual leader.) The field was freshly mowed, and we sat in camp chairs, circled about him as he prepared to impart valuable wisdom.

I didn't mind Sundays so much. After getting through my father's two- to three-hour sermons (most of which I was able to tune out with a storyline I made up in my head), I usually had the rest of the day to myself. I could read. Nap. Write. We weren't supposed to work on Sundays, so there was no danger of my father asking us to do construction work on the house.

But after that Sunday, that particular Sunday, my life would never be the same.

The Smiths were a pillar family in the patriarchal movement. Those who upheld the teaching of this movement believed they were doing things God's way, following an orthodox path. Fathers were the heads of the home. Mothers were the helpmeets. Children were a gift from the Lord. The more children a family had, the more blessed they were by God. I heard many a sermon shaming those who chose to only have two or three children. Most in the movement believed the way Christians would take over the world was by having children and training them in the way of the Lord. Then those children would have children and the apostates and the lukewarm would die out, because families of two or three children had nothing on our family of seven.

These teachings were powerful. They were motivating. I wanted to be a part of this movement to take over the world, and I was happy to play my part.

But my family was not part of this movement yet. Not until that Sunday. My parents had spent the previous evening at the home of my best friend, Anne, with her family and their houseguests, the Smiths. The Smiths were also good friends with Anne's family and were held in high regard in the homeschool community, considering they had raised four godly now-adult children.

None of the adult children were married at that time, and that was a little strange considering how important marriage was in the movement. But it was a small matter. We could all easily believe the Lord was saving them for someone special—or there was no one good enough for them.

The day following this meeting, my father held court in the field. The sermon was short and more a moment for my father to announce our family was taking a new direction. Since women were meant to be wives and mothers, a helpmeet to her husband and caretakers of children, here was no need for them to go to college. In fact, it was a waste of time. All the daughters of our family would stay home and serve their father until they married, the same way Susan Smith served her father. At the time, she was unmarried in her thirties.

My father was very proud of this new plan. He announced it as if it were the answer he'd been searching for all along. (It probably was.)

And my heart sank so deep in my stomach I thought I might throw up.

I had not realized it until then, but I was biding my time. Biding it until I graduated high school at eighteen and disappeared to college. I hadn't realized how much I was looking forward to the freedom of adulthood until that freedom was ripped from my hands following one conversation.

Right then and there, I started to cry. I said desperately, "How will I ever meet a husband if I don't go to college?"

My father's face changed from one of glee to one of anger. He said, how dare I cry because I didn't know how I'd find a husband with-out college? Was God not big enough to provide, as long as we were pleasing him?

I could see my siblings all around me, sinking deeper into their camp chairs, making themselves small so as not to get caught in the ripple of my father's rage.

He continued, saying it was my fault I had ever planned to go to college in the first place. He had never told me I would go to college. I'd made it up in my mind that college was in the plan.

I distinctly remember in that moment flashing back to my sixteenth birthday a few months earlier. My mother had helped me pick out a camera (the kind with film) and had said she wanted me to have a good camera, one I could take with me to college.

Everyone went to college. It was part of the circle of life.

My greatest sin in the following years was the sin of filling in the blanks. Assuming something my father had never said. If my father didn't tell me what to think about something, I'd decide what I thought on my own. Then my father would shame or punish me for making a decision for myself without speaking to him.

We'd dance this dance for ten years.

But in that moment, I didn't blame my father. I was conditioned to believe he was always right. So I did what I always did: shoved my desire down deep, watching as so many expectations turned to ash that floated away at a gust of wind.

I imagined once or twice inventing a device that allowed me to go back in time so I could puncture the tires of my parents' car so they wouldn't go meet with the Smiths.

But I couldn't blame the Smiths, either. The movement itself was a subset of the homeschool movement. My parents were bound to encounter the teaching. And my father had been waiting for just the right thing that would allow him to take absolute control of his family.

He'd finally found it.

ARRANGED MARRIAGES

I saw the life that could have been mine flash before my eyes. As I listened to a *Bare Marriage* podcast episode on my couch in the safety of my apartment (thirty-eight years old and unmarried), I gripped a pillow, recognizing how narrowly I had escaped Alyssa's fate.

Alyssa Wakefield married a Welch, one of the families I hold responsible for my father's foray into the world of the Christian patriarchy movement. In her interview with podcast host Sheila Gregoire, she described her arranged marriage. She wasn't interested in the man who became her husband, but her father was so excited about the match that he forced her into being alone with him, abandoning her one evening. At nineteen, Alyssa hadn't been allowed to date. She hadn't really been allowed to speak to men. Yet there she was, alone with a man her father wanted her to marry as he talked about his dreams for the future.

According to Alyssa, before they became engaged, she exchanged only six letters with her intended, where most of the content contained her future husband's exposition on his views and beliefs.

After they married, Alyssa endured nineteen years of abuse, allegedly functioning as her husband's in-home sex worker to meet his appetites, birthing eight children, and sometimes starving because her husband couldn't afford the number of mouths he had to feed. Alyssa finally recognized how much of her life she'd dedicated to honoring her father, even enduring an arranged marriage because she was told it was pleasing to God that she endure. Eventually, she divorced her husband and at the time of the podcast interview was carving out a life of healing for herself and her eight children.

I knew the Welches as a teenager. They contributed to the reason my sisters and I were not allowed to go to college. They supported my father's vision for creating a home-grown incubator of self-gratification from his wife and children, demonstrating how to do this in the name of God.

I used to have dreams about my father forcing me to marry someone. There was one dream I entertained my family with where my father picked my husband. Just before the wedding, a hurricane came and destroyed the house, the church, and my ugly wedding dress. My family laughed when I shared the dream.

Today, I salute the powers of my subconscious mind for conjuring a natural disaster to get out of marriage. I don't believe these dreams were disjointed fabrications of my imagination. It was the water we swam in.

A childhood friend of mine almost married into one of the Pillars of Patriarchy families. She felt pressure from her parents and the community surrounding us. Yet just when an engagement seemed imminent, her prospect broke up with her.

Over a decade later, my friend admits she hadn't been in love with him, but he'd been the sort of person she imagined she would end up with. The sort of person she knew her parents would love. While her father hadn't abandoned her and told her it was God's will to marry the man, her parents' excitement had almost sealed her in a fate that could have ended similarly to Alyssa's. If not in divorce, in a lifetime of unhappiness.

I used to fear I'd be forced to marry someone like my father. Indeed, someone like my father was the only sort of person my father would likely have approved of. Yet my father never put pressure on me to marry anyone specifically. In fact, I sometimes wonder if he wanted his daughters to get married at all, as he made it incredibly difficult for us to even be friends with guys, including barring us from college, the place many in the South encounter their future spouses.

Maybe he only ever wanted to keep us for himself.

WRONG SORT OF WOMAN

After that Sunday when my father announced my sisters and I would not go to college, our family adopted a pretty extreme version of patriarchy. When I tell my story, most Christians are appropriately appalled at how much control my father had over my life. With a growing awareness of cults and an increased under-standing of the trauma caused by spiritual abuse, most churchgoers don't have difficulty acknowledging my upbringing as abusive.

However, when I attempt to draw a comparison to common Christian teachings and messages about marriage and gender, I often lose my audience. I believe this is because the gender and marriage hierarchy is more subtle in evangelicalism, but it's very much still there.

I managed to escape my parents' home when I was in my mid-twenties (more on that later). My first step toward a vocation in full-time ministry was moving to Mexico to work with a church plant. I spent over a year raising the funds stateside before joining up with the mission team starting the church.

When I'd completed my year, my representative with the orga-nization that sent me to Mexico wanted to do an exit interview. She specifically wanted to know what my experience was like as a single woman, as she was a single woman considering going on the mission field for four years. She assured me the mission organiza-tion was interested in making missions more accessible, as many single women seemed to struggle with finding a place in the field.

In later years, returning to the mission field was an optional career path. I think I assumed I'd go back, and I pursued education and training with that end in mind. Ultimately, I decided not to go back *because* I was a single woman. Though I loved many things about Mexico, the patriarchal culture of Mexico mixed with the patriarchal culture of the mission industry confirmed for me that if I was going to continue to make progress in my healing after leaving my family, I couldn't be somewhere that resembled it.

The mission team leader in Mexico could be very kind, charming, and friendly.

He could also be entitled and domineering.

During the first few months, I cried so many times because of things he said to me. Once, he asked me to reach out to the teenage daughter of someone attending the church. I managed to get her information and text her a few times, but she did not text back. Considering the cultural barriers, I did not want to keep pushing. Clearly, she wasn't interested in responding to me.

Months later, the team leader brought this up. "I told you to reach out to her and you just decided on your own that you weren't going to."

I defended myself. "I did reach out to her. She didn't respond."

"I don't care. I told you to reach out, so you keep doing it until I say it's okay to stop."

Got it. He preferred robotic obedience, not common sense. No nuance.

My coworker, a married man named Jeff and also a missionary, told me his first two years had been a struggle. It felt like he had to prove himself to our team leader. After two years, things got better for him. I didn't have two years, but at least my team leader wasn't domineering because I was a woman; he was that way to everyone. Silver linings.

Jeff was only a few years older than I was, but he was invited to the planning meeting for a new church plant. I wasn't invited to that planning meeting. Even now, I believe if I'd been a man, or married, I would have been invited.

I know this because Julia, Jeff's wife, had also been invited. Julia didn't work in the team office, yet she'd been included because her status as a married woman superseded my status, even though I was in the office every day, just like Jeff. (Nobody ever said this out loud. It was all in the optics.)

Despite my self-absorbed team leader, I loved working in Mexico. Sunday mornings were my favorite. I'd sometimes drive through a Starbucks on my way to church. (Starbucks in Mexico tastes better than Starbucks in the States.) The church plant met in the upper room of a restaurant. I'd arrive about half an hour before the start of the service. Even though I hadn't been invited to the planning meeting, I was considered part of the church planting team, so I needed to be there early to set up and help get the coffee going.

That little church plant sang songs in Spanish, but the sermons were in both English and Spanish, depending on who was preaching (always one of the male missionaries, never a woman). One of the draws for the community was that folks could attend this church to practice English. Most of the kids who attended went to English-speaking schools.

The first thing that a church plant needs is someone to preach a sermon. The next thing is someone to lead the music. The third most important thing is someone to lead the children's church so the parents can worship undistracted.

The minute the planning team started discussing who would lead the children's church, I leaned hard into my non-planning-team status and made it very clear I would *not* lead children's church. I was willing to go to a different church to avoid this task, even if it made sense that job would fall to me, the single woman and the obvious choice, since what else was I good for?

But I would not be the default teacher simply because they didn't know what else to do with me. In fact, during my time attending that church, I didn't volunteer once. I knew how these things worked. The minute I showed any sign of being moderately willing to participate, the whole responsibility would fall to me. I avoided it like I'd avoid a pock-faced suitor with sweaty palms.

The job ended up falling to Julia. I felt no guilt. She was a part of the *real* planning team, after all. It also made perfect sense to me that the people with kids would be the ones to lead the children's church. The person without kids should not have to carry that burden, unless, of course, they actually want to.

But the church often likes to guilt childless people into doing this work as a service to the ones with kids. If married people superseded single people, parents superseded the childless.

I loved kids. I enjoyed hanging out with them and goofing off with them. I even volunteered to babysit Jeff and Julia's kids a couple times a month. But I also loved the church service and felt it a great injustice that I should have to sacrifice that when I was child-free. I resented the assumption that just because I was a woman it meant I wanted to be around kids all the time.

For the next year, I made myself useful in other ways and successfully avoided teaching children's church.

Attending church and leading Bible studies were both part of my job. I loved it. I loved leading the short-term mission trips from the States that came down throughout the year and over the summer. I met so many people that year in Mexico. My email list doubled. It was high-energy, people-oriented work, and there were many times when I was leading and coordinating the teams that I felt like I was working directly in my wheelhouse.

I'd never felt this way before—about any job I'd ever had. I'd been led to believe you would never enjoy work, yet here I was, liking my job.

I began to wonder if my father and the community of my patriarchal upbringing led me to believe work was terrible as a way to frighten me away from a career. They used the third chapter of Genesis to say that work was meant to be difficult. After Adam and Eve ate the fruit of the forbidden tree, God cursed the ground, saying Adam would labor and toil. God cursed Eve by saying she needed to submit to her husband and that childbirth would be painful. Those around me said work outside the home was only for husbands. If a wife worked, she was double-cursing herself, because her curse was in submitting to her husband and having pain in childbirth—not a career. Why would a woman ever do this to herself?

No one in the Christian patriarchy movement had a category for, or knew what God said about, a woman who wasn't a wife. The implied best option was to never get in that situation in the first place. Just get married so you don't have to worry about what happens if you remain unmarried longer than you are supposed to.

Later, when I was on the mission field, or in the evangelical churches I attended or worked for, no one ever said this outright, but the feeling that I was out of place as a single woman never disappeared. This was true even after I left the Christian patriarchy movement. It could be that in both my family of origin and the evangelical church, the inability to fully accept a single woman is rooted in Genesis chapter three. The Bible doesn't provide regulations for this sort of woman, because this woman isn't supposed to exist.

DANGEROUS

I believed if you reached your thirties without getting married, you were doomed to a life of spinsterhood. "Set aside by God for special service" was the consolation prize for the runner-up women who couldn't lock down a man.

After crawling my way out of that world, one that told me my worth lay in my ability to secure a husband to be my spiritual leader, I thought I found a church where my freedom was guaranteed, only to awaken inside evangelicalism—a church culture with the same values as my ultraconservative upbringing (they were just less overt about it). They valued women who were married and birthing babies. I wasn't that sort of woman. Much worse, I wasn't actively seeking to *be* that sort of woman. I quickly discovered the only sort of single person you were really allowed to be was the sort pining after marriage and regularly begging God, and begging friends to beg God on your behalf, to find you a husband.

Maybe the folks in my mainstream evangelical church weren't looking at me, in my mid-thirties, as if I were a poor sop who'd missed the marriage train. However, I did experience the cruel cut of silence and exclusion. They didn't know what to do with me. They couldn't just be friends with me (what would we even talk about?). But they also couldn't treat me like a younger woman who they needed to mentor (because many of the married couples in my church were my age or younger). It would have been so much easier for them (and for me) if marriage was on my mind the way it was supposed to be.

I am so much more interesting than my marital status, but I consistently experienced this as a problem. The problem wasn't that I was unmarried. The problem was that I wasn't working very hard to change it. As the years progressed, rather than growing more discontented with my status, I seemed to grow more and more… happy.

Wait, this was not the way singleness was supposed to work. You weren't supposed to *like* it. Tolerate it, sure. Be content—that was definitely godly. But find it a suitable lifestyle you had no interest in changing? I can almost hear Sharpay from *High School*

Musical belting, "Stick to the status quo!" as her vocal cords strain with panic.

As I became more confident in expressing how much I enjoyed being single, I experienced pushback from both sides. The married women assured me I just hadn't met the right one yet. The single women seemed to think I'd betrayed them in some way or that I was just pretending as a way of denying reality.

All the while I started to wonder if the ones living in denial were the ones trapped inside the system. I don't mean the marriage system. I mean the system that subtly (and not-so-subtly) championed marriage as a prize worth attaining and striving for. Something women gave up careers for, sacrificed their well-being for, ignored their instincts for, rushed into before they were ready, and bemoaned when they didn't have it.

I don't see marriage as the problem. The problem is that in both the Christian patriarchy movement and mainstream evangelicalism, marriage is presented as the default. The expectation. The assumed path. The better path. Singleness is an accident, not an option.

Throughout my adult life, I just wanted someone to tell me it was okay to be single. I wanted someone to assure me that I could live a thriving, vibrant life all on my own. I wanted people to present marriage as an option I could choose if I wanted, but no one would doubt my sanity, my worth, or my maturity if I chose something different.

The person who finally bucked up and followed through on this message was me. Church culture—and the wider Western culture influenced by church culture—isn't championing this message. And it's done a lot of damage to women. It is extremely difficult to grow up indoctrinated with marriage as God's best and then live a life of solo pleasure. It's extremely difficult to not doubt your worth when you've been conditioned to believe your worth comes from marriage or the pursuit of marriage.

I believe there is an underlying thread to church culture that has a vested interest in silencing the message that living a thriving single life is a legitimate option. The patriarchal culture of evangelical Christianity needs marriage in order to work. Single women, unattached to a man, are extremely dangerous to the foundation of patriarchy. So, rest assured, if you experience fear when you think about yourself or someone you know living their life without marriage, that feeling likely has a root. If women aren't bound to a man through marriage, the route to control begins to break down

EQUALITY

"I'm not going to be a pastor's wife," I said. "*I* am going to be the pastor. He gets to marry *me*."

A year after Mexico, at the beginnings of my career with the institutional church, I was single, attending seminary, and working part-time in youth ministry. Before I left for seminary and even during seminary, a few people hinted that I was attending seminary to find myself a pastor to marry.

I shut this thinking down with all the swiftness of Electra's blade, informing each person who dared to suggest this that I intended to be the pastor, married to someone who supported my vocation. I hadn't yet figured out how I was going to achieve this, since the denomination I worked for didn't allow female pastors. But they'd promised me that women were equal to men, and I believed I'd get to function as a pastor, even if I didn't get to carry the title.

One of my first hints that gender equality was a false promise was a moment when I was telling my boss at the youth ministry that I wished the church would invest in women the same way it invested in and mentored men. I was speaking generally but (not-so-subtly) hinting that I resented how much time my boss spent with my male counterpart when I was also a seminary student, planning to go into ministry as a full-time profession.

My boss hemmed and hawed for several minutes, but the gist of his response was "Sometimes it's challenging to put a lot of time into mentoring women when usually they do not stay in ministry after they get married and have children."

It took me a couple years to rightfully be indignant about this stance. First, it is entirely demeaning to mothers. A woman isn't worth the investment because she's *just* going to be a mom?

Second, I shouldn't have had to prove I would stay in ministry forever in order to deserve the same investment the church was giving to men. If they really valued women equally, why weren't they giving me equal attention and care?

In the community I grew up in, they emphasized the superiority of men over women. I mean, at least they were open about it, right? In evangelicalism, the messages of the system also support this belief—only they try to convince you men and women are equal *and as long as they are each serving in their proper roles*, everyone will be happy and living a biblical life.

It was very convincing. I believed them for nearly a decade.

Here's the truth: The value is not equal. There is a hierarchy among genders, marital statuses, and sexual orientations. It isn't equality. It is the system's way to maintain control by categorizing people based on their perceived value.

TWO: CONTROL

How to Keep People Dependent

HOW TO BE A CULT LEADER

If you want to be a cult leader—or any sort of authoritarian leader—here are the steps:

Step One: Join a community that conditions everyone to rely on a source outside of themselves for direction, advice, and affirmation. This is easiest if the outside source is a deity they cannot see. All you have to do is claim to speak for that deity. Then, if they ever question you, you can deflect that questioning back onto the deity.

Say something like this: "It's not me who's saying this. It's God. I know it's difficult. It's difficult for me, too. But this is what the Lord says. Let's trust God together." With this, you have achieved three things. First, you've shifted the responsibility and blame to the higher power. Second, you've supported a viewpoint that following the deity is difficult, therefore normalizing difficulty as a sign of trusting God. Finally, you've created a dynamic of empathy and solidarity between yourself and the target. They see you as one of them, struggling alongside them to do the right thing. They will never know you are controlling them.

Step Two: Teach your followers to mistrust themselves (specifically, their desires). This does not have to be too dramatic. Simply point them toward the deity whenever they share an inkling of want. Encourage them to seek the Lord's guidance and to not trust their own heart. Teach them to surrender their dreams to the deity, offering it as a fragrant sacrifice. Teach them to be joyful when they give up their dreams for God. Teach them that wanting something too much is dangerous. Blame their selfish desires whenever something doesn't work out the way they want it to. Tell them God is teaching them a lesson. Plant the idea that they must not have heard God correctly or prayed hard enough or that their desires were never from God to begin with. Teach them to fear happiness by telling them that God does not want them to be happy—God wants them to be holy.

Step Three: Keep them away from outside influences. It might not be feasible to separate them geographically. Society typically frowns upon communes. The more normal your community looks, the easier it will be to hide in plain sight. But that doesn't mean you cannot remain their primary influence. You do this by feeding mistrust of anyone and anything that doesn't sound like you. Shame them for watching films that celebrate self-expression and independence. Reward them when they read books about missionaries who make sacrifices for the kingdom of heaven. Dole out praise—sparingly, however, so your followers will be grateful whenever they receive it. Condition them to feel safe around people who think like you. Condition them to fear anything that is different.

Step Four: Build on step three by giving them a common enemy. I suggest making that common enemy anything that is traditionally considered feminine—for example, female bodies, emotions, and art. This is easiest because a lot of this mistrust is already embedded into society at large. You won't have to work very hard. Teach emotional control, vilify art that provokes critical thought, and shame the female body. These things will occupy the minds of your followers so much it will distract them from their true enemy: you.

This approach will also allow a certain type of person to rise more easily to the top. Men, for example. If one demographic feels like they have power in this community without having to work too hard for it, then you'll have ready allies. They will fight for these principles on your behalf. Eventually, all you'll have to do is sit back and watch.

This, my friend, is how you become a cult leader. Enjoy.

WANT

Aside from the normal human struggle of choosing a profession, I had the dark angel of cult influence flitting around my head, continuously mocking me for daring to think I could have a career. In my mid-twenties, I had a very difficult time deciding what I was going to do with my life. I constantly worried people would find out where I was from. They'd wonder why I finished college at twenty-six or why my résumé was so sparse. Though my CV reflected oppression and abuse, I couldn't say that in a job interview where I wanted to leave prospective employers with a happy feeling.

Our culture conditions women to downplay their gifts and work only for what they need, rather than what they want or deserve. Add to that dynamic an upbringing that told me God did not design me for a career. God designed me for bearing children and helping my husband with the vision God gave him (because God only gives visions to men). Women with careers worked outside the created order, referencing the first part of Genesis where Eve was presumably created to be Adam's helper.

For a few years after my older brother Micah got married, before he and his wife had children, my sister-in-law worked in a clothing boutique. She was only working part time, but my parents still made comments on our way home after visiting them that my sister-in-law was skirting a dangerous line by having an authority (her boss) who wasn't her husband.

I found this judgment confusing, considering my sisters and I all had jobs. They were part-time and fulfilled my father's criteria that the jobs be flexible so we could be on call for him whenever he needed us. How was it different for my sister-in-law? Did my parents' comments mean when my sisters and I were married, we shouldn't work at all? Even if we didn't have children? Was my sister-in-law just supposed to sit at home, tending to domestic duties while her husband was away at work? Did marriage magically make any sort of income outside of your husband's paycheck a threat to the marriage?

Following this line of reasoning, I heard from my father, and the conservative Christian sermons on cassette tapes we listened to as a family, that the reason for the increased number of divorces and the breakdown of Christian marriages was directly related to the education and career orientation of women. These messages pitted a woman's career against her duty to her husband. If a woman had independence and the ability to support herself, what was to stop her from leaving her husband the moment she became discontented?

That there are legitimate reasons for a woman to leave her husband, such as abuse or infidelity, were presented as uncommon and the worst-case scenario. My father scoffed at a father of another acquaintance who raised his daughters to prepare for the three *D*'s: Death, Divorce, and Disability. This father still believed husbands should be primary breadwinners but also believed women should be equipped for the possibility of extenuating circumstances. Conversely, my father thought it was a waste of time and money for a woman to invest four years and thousands of dollars in an education that would prepare her for a very unlikely possibility.

"Very unlikely," he said. Yet he'd married a woman (my mother) who'd been raised by a single mom. Nana had gone to college in the '50s, even though her parents were not fully supportive of a woman having higher education. She stopped work for a few years after she got married but returned when her husband died of cancer. She raised two daughters with the income from teaching and a military pension from my grandfather's death.

I once presented this loophole to my father, considering one of the three *D*'s was a reality in our family tree.

My father responded that my grandmother could have supported herself and two daughters on my grandfather's pension alone. She hadn't needed to work. In fact, her career was likely the reason she never remarried. She hadn't *needed* a husband, so she never got one.

Never mind Nana had a career the first time around and actually met her husband at her first teaching job. Never mind that in the aftermath of her husband's death, she still had two young daughters to care for, the presence of whom might have been a greater deterrent to finding a new committed relationship than her job. Never mind that it seemed the main motivation for a woman to get married and stay married was because she had no other options.

In the Christian patriarchy movement, there isn't a category for a woman to have dreams and pursue a career because she wants to. The only career a woman should want is one supporting her husband and raising children for the kingdom of God.

Still, there was an expectation in our family that the unmarried adult daughters would do *something* with our time. We had financial clarity on this as my parents paid for basic room and board, but anything extra (including clothing and gas for the car), we were expected to pay for ourselves.

I still get a hitch in my stomach and feel constriction in my chest when I think about one of my jobs, which was cleaning houses. It was good money, considering the little income I needed, but I hated it. Literally hated it.

I know now I hated it because I am an intellectual creative. This job was the opposite of *me*. But who I was and what I wanted did not fit with the domesticity expected from me because of a verse in chapter two of the book of Titus that said women should be "sensible, pure, workers at home."

In her early twenties, my sister Joann got approval to move out of my parents' house and into a townhome with some friends. She is two years younger than me. Her source of income was a job at a florist shop and a side hustle planning events. Flowers and events were acceptable professions. She had a skill and was able to be independent and control her own schedule, so she could stop when she got married or continue working at a job that allowed her the flexibility to serve and support her husband. With this job setup, my father still remained head of her household, justification for which he derived from Numbers 30:3–5.

*When a young woman still living in her father's household
makes a vow to the LORD or obligates herself by a pledge and
her father hears about her vow or pledge but says nothing to
her, then all her vows and every pledge by which she obligated
herself will stand. But if her father forbids her when he hears
about it, none of her vows or the pledges by which she obligated
herself will stand; the LORD will release her because her father
has forbidden her.*

According to my father, these verses also supported the belief
that a woman must always be under the authority of a man, as the
Bible never divulges regulations for an unmarried woman (unless
she is a widow, but let's not get ahead of ourselves). Ergo, implied
perpetual male authority.

There's also a chance my father approved working with flowers
for Joann because this path is stereotypically feminine. But I don't
have any evidence to back this up.

A couple years later, my sister Macey became certified as a
personal trainer. Her gig was the same deal: flexible, and she
controlled her own schedule. My father also valued exercise. He
thought Macey could be a force for good, preventing her friends
from getting fat after they got married and had babies (this is not
hyperbole).

All of this helped me understand a profession itself wasn't
against the rules. The profession just needed to fall within a specific
category to receive my father's approval. But nothing I wanted to
do fit in those categories.

In the meantime, I dabbled in things my father valued, hoping
one of these pursuits would stick. I taught Spanish and worked
as a tutor for homeschool kids when their parents were losing
patience with a specific subject. Most of the time, I was counting
the minutes until the one-hour class was over and guzzling coffee
so I wouldn't fall asleep. I was bored out of my mind.

For about a year after high school, I worked as the front desk assistant for my father's company. While it was steady work and a decent income, it also fed my coffee addiction. I struggled to focus, but I just thought I was lazy. I went to the bathroom nearly every hour because I needed an excuse to get up and walk. My father presented me with different options for learning software that would fill my time, but I just grew frustrated and felt like I was doing algebra. I hated algebra.

This job, I discovered too late, put me in further contact with my father. A number of times my father would be so angry at my work or my response to an email that he'd make his way up to the front desk to chastise me. Then I'd also have to endure his sour mood on the ride home from work.

To my relief, I got a summer job babysitting. I worked every morning so I couldn't go to work with my father. This job was much better suited to me as I could spend most of my days at the pool with the kids and I could read while the youngest took a nap and the older kids were playing at the neighbors'. When the summer ended, I did not return to my father's workplace.

The only part of working at my father's company I remember with positivity is the day the marketing manager told me I had a good voice. He asked me if I'd read some voice-over scripts for a few promotional videos. I got paid to do something that sort of resembled acting. I was thrilled.

And someone told me I had a good voice, which wasn't something I'd ever thought could be *good*. I'd never in my life been asked to do something because I had natural talent. I rarely got accolades of any kind. I believe now it wasn't because I wasn't good at anything. I think it was because what I was good at did not appeal to my family culture.

As a child, I attended shows at the local community theater with Nana. I'd hold on to the playbills, which always had the dates for the next auditions on the back flap. I'd put the auditions on our family calendar and ask Nana to drive me. I was eleven when this frenzy started. I auditioned for thirteen plays before I was cast in a small role. I kept seeking and creating opportunities all through high school and performed in a production the year after I graduated high school.

That play was the only thing that made me happy, the only purpose I had after graduation.

It was also my last performance.

I look back on that season and wonder why I quit. For starters, I believe it had something to do with the time commitment. It was a lot of work, with several rehearsals a week on top of multiple performances on the weekends the show was running. My responsibilities to my family did not end simply because I was in a show. Every Saturday, everyone living at home had to do construction work on the house, building my father's mansion, so I had to get special permission from him to be in shows. I'd go to rehearsal in the mornings, then I'd get home, change into work clothes, and join the rest of the family in working on the house.

I'd also grown up with parents who limited their children's outside-of-family activities because they were seen as a distraction, taking away time from what was most important: family life. My father valued family dinner, so we had to ask permission for anything that would make us miss the meal. We'd have better odds of getting his blessing if our activities happened after dinner so we could still be home for family time. I think the only reason my parents allowed theater was because they felt sorry for me for not having a "thing." I was also so incredibly passionate about it and showed so much initiative at a very young age, it would have been cruel, even by their standards, to not give me a shot.

I recall this posture toward the family unit—one of always turning toward it, keeping your feet rooted in it—was held up as the biblical, most godly way. God came first, the father second, and the wife and children fell beneath that. My father couldn't lead, direct, and protect his family if he didn't have his family close, so we had to be together as much as possible.

Part of me knew if I continued down the theater route, eventually it would become a battle. My father indulged my passion because I didn't have anything else, but I predicted that wouldn't last long. It was better to do something that would allow me to fly under the radar. An activity like theater would constantly cast a spotlight on my time away from my family.

Ultimately, I stopped auditioning because I was worn out from navigating the family rules and obligations that competed with my passion. Would theater help me be a wife and mom? I couldn't see a way to justify it.

It was also easier and less painful to stop before this thing I loved was taken away—something my instincts told me was inevitable.

In the end, my pursuit of theater died a silent death, mourned privately by only one person: me.

BREATHE

We call it the sibling gossip chain. When one sibling finds out something important, they tell another. Then that sibling tells another until eventually all the siblings know, as if they were all there.

This is how chains work. But it isn't gossip if it's true.

I received two revelations from the sibling gossip chain, years after I'd moved away from my hometown. At a dinner with some once-removed cousins, my father said I was the child who got spanked the least out of all the kids, adding, "I should have spanked her more."

Apparently, he also said, "I should have never let her go to Guatemala."

This statement I wholeheartedly agree with. If he had any intention of maintaining control of me, keeping me fearful, submissive, and exactly where he wanted me, he should have never let me go to Guatemala.

His decision to let me go to Guatemala when I was nineteen did not make sense to outsiders. If he wouldn't let me go to college or have a career, why did he let me go to Guatemala?

I'll try to explain.

It was the principle of college, the idea you were preparing for a career you would never have, that made college forbidden. It was also the length of time and the amount of money. Again, why waste four years and thousands upon thousands of dollars, possibly going into debt, when you were just going to get married and have babies?

Look at your mother. She has no career. At least the GI bill from her father's time in the military paid for her school so she didn't give her husband debt as a wedding gift. Other than meeting her husband, college was a complete waste of time. Your mother couldn't get a job right now if she tried. College did nothing for your mother; God can provide a husband without college. Don't be stupid and go to school just to get a husband.

Guatemala was a different story. First, I was only going for about six weeks. Three of those weeks, I'd be in one town at language school by myself. The other three weeks, I'd be in another town with missionary friends, and Macey and Joann would be joining us.

Still, those first three weeks were a concern. I was under instructions from my father to find a way to call home every week—this was before any sort of video call or global cell phone plan. They bought me a calling card to use on a landline.

We weren't sure what sort of internet access I'd have, so the phone call was the only stipulation. I eventually found an internet café where I could take my thumb drive of responses to emails, dial up, copy, paste, and then dial down—for a couple of dollars. I communicated with friends and siblings through email. But my parents only got a phone call.

My father accompanied me to Quezaltenango to see the school and meet my host family. I was incredibly grateful for the support, as I was only nineteen and this truly was the longest I'd been away from home by myself.

That first night in Quezaltenango, we had dinner in a restaurant with live music. I used my digital camera to record the performance. Already enthralled with the language and culture, I couldn't believe I'd be living in this city for three weeks.

The morning before my father left, we went to the town square and got ice cream at a McDonald's. A McDonald's outside of the USA is a luxury. The food tastes so much better. Then my father hopped on a bus to go back to the airport in Guatemala City, and I tried not to cry. For the first time in my life, I felt truly alone.

Another reason I believe my parents were okay with Guatemala is learning Spanish was one skill my father approved of. He had always wanted to learn another language, so having a daughter who could speak Spanish was second best.

I also think they'd noticed my despondency the year after I graduated from high school. I now know I was deep in a season of depression, something that has come in waves throughout my whole life, but, as a family, we did not believe in depression. I was taught that "people who trust God do not get depressed."

I think they wanted me to have something to look forward to. Maybe deep down in the cavern of their hearts, they wanted me to be happy. Or at least, they did not want me to be miserable.

But years later, when my father said he should have never let me go to Guatemala, he was absolutely right. Guatemala changed my life. I would never be the same after that experience.

LIES

I uncovered three lies in Guatemala.

Lie Number One: Christians are the only good people and only people in the world you can really trust.

Lie Number Two: Christians are the only true friends you will ever have because they are the only people you really have anything in common with.

Lie Number Three: You cannot survive, or be happy, without your family.

The thing about attending language school in another country is that unless you go there with a school group or a church group, you're usually there by yourself—which means everyone else is there by themselves. You can make friends in a short time because nobody has any other distractions. You instantly have several things in common with everyone at school: five hours of classes every day, living in a foreign country, a host family you can't communicate with, fear of parasites from fresh food, a list of favorite restaurants and coffee shops you have discovered.

Armed with this common ground, you quickly migrate to one another and start meeting up after class to study, which translates to talking about all the things you miss from home (even though you've only been gone a few days). You read books in English that other students left behind, because your mind is lumpy from speaking Spanish. Yes, you should be practicing with your classmates, but your brain is so exhausted you can't seem to even string English words together.

On a weekend, you take a big excursion to the mall, each paying a few quetzales for a bus ride. You see a doubleheader of American films with Spanish subtitles and cackle at how cheap the popcorn and soda are. You never buy popcorn and soda at theaters in the States.

On the next weekend, your little band of classmates signs up for an organized school event to the hot springs. Transportation is a chicken bus (a school bus packed with literally anything, from humans to produce to goats to squawking chickens). The bus can't make it up the mountain, so you climb into the bed of a pickup truck and giggle because it's definitely illegal to ride in the back of a pickup, on the open road, in the U.S.

After a dip in the hot springs, you enjoy a cup of hot chocolate (made with real melted chocolate—none of that powder stuff) before heading back to the city, the reverse of how you came.

The next weekend, you plan to do a night hike of a live volcano, but it gets canceled because the eruption of lava has gotten a little too dangerous.

None of your new friends are Christians. They cuss a lot. Most of them are humanitarians, doing work to improve agriculture or living conditions in other coun-tries. One person is from the Peace Corps. One is a film director from Hollywood. One is a crew member of a yacht, taking a few weeks off to learn some Spanish before joining another assignment.

In a few days, you'll be getting back on the bus to Guatemala City to meet up with the missionaries and your sisters. You take a notebook around to all your classmates to gather their email addresses (this is before social media). On your last day of class, you get photos with your teachers, your new friends, and your host family. You realize you're fighting tears again. But this time they are tears because you don't want to go home.

But to admit that, to even think about that, would be the worst thing ever.

OXYGEN

Guatemala changed my life because it was the first time I could really breathe. The sleeping, almost-dead girl inside of me opened her eyes. She stretched and yawned and inhaled oxygen.

I'd never known what breathing was like before.

I believe my breathing came easy because of how difficult it was to communicate with home from a foreign country. If I'd gone to Central America about eight years later, I would have been able to call home more often. It would have been easier to email. Even just a couple years later, Skype and Wi-Fi joined the technological scene.

But for the short time I was there, I really couldn't talk to my parents much. And I didn't miss them, or home, nearly as much as I was supposed to.

This was the first crack in the structure. Fissures began to form. The foundation was suddenly unstable. I never in my life imagined I wouldn't want to go home or that my family wouldn't be the most important thing.

I rarely imagined a future outside of my hometown in the South where I didn't live just a few houses down from my parents or in a neighborhood a couple miles away. I started to think, *What if I lived in Guatemala? What if I became a missionary? What if I moved far away?*

The light fueled by the oxygen must have shown through my eyes, because that first night at home my father did his best to put it out.

Everyone was so excited to have me back. We ate dinner on the back porch, burgers straight off the grill. My sisters and I told stories about our time with the missionaries, shared stories because we had all been there together.

No one asked me about school. Indeed, the memories of school were already starting to fade.

As dinner wound down, my siblings stood to start clearing away the dishes, but I stayed at the table, looking at my plate. Maybe I wanted to talk to my parents about school. Maybe I was tired. Maybe I just forgot how to jump up and clean the minute dinner finished. I must have lingered too long.

"Katherine, help clean the kitchen." The sharpness in my father's tone and the steel look of command in his eyes communicated clearly what he wanted: *Don't start thinking you don't have to work just because we let you go away for a few weeks.*

I stood to help with the cleaning, squeezing my eyes against the sting of tears.

He wanted to reel me back in, place me back in my role of helpful oldest daughter. *Don't forget whose daughter you are.* The ground rules had been set: Don't make him regret giving you some freedom. Fall back into the old ways. Be good and humble and hardworking.

But if he wanted me to be happy I was home, his words had the opposite effect. I was only home a few hours before wishing I was back in Guatemala.

DANGEROUS DESIRES

I really wasn't allowed to have my own hopes and dreams for most of my life. As a result, my relationship with desire has always been complicated. I was conditioned to always search for God's will, to align my desires with the Lord's. Proverbs 3:5–6 says, "Trust in the LORD with all your heart and do not lean on your own understanding; in all your ways acknowledge Him, and He will make your paths straight."

I was taught that if we trusted the Lord by surrendering our dreams and desires to him, then he would direct us where he wanted us to go.

I do not remember in all my childhood, teenhood, or young adult years ever being told that maybe my desires—whatever they were—might actually come from God in the first place. I believed my desires, at their core, were selfish and untrustworthy. The intensity of my longing was only an indicator of how far from God I had strayed. If I wanted something too badly, God would not give it to me in order to make sure my heart was fully his.

If I wanted something and my desire did not come to fruition, it was a sign that God did not want it for me. I must joyfully give up that desire in response to his will.

The more grateful we could be in the loss of our dream, the more we blessed God in our sorrow and the more holy we were.

We were allowed to be sad—we just had to make sure we were sad like Job was sad. He tore his clothes, covered himself in ashes, and then cried out, "The LORD gave and the LORD has taken away. Blessed be the name of the LORD."

A friend told me a story once about the time she and her partner took a big risk to start her own business. They ended up putting a lot on credit and then her partner lost their job. Because of their significant debt, they ended up having to move into her parents' basement and find jobs doing things they didn't want to do.

She struggled with this season because she'd had so much faith. She believed God would come through for them, as they prayed fervently. She knew God was on her side.

But when the result was homelessness, it caused her to struggle with taking risks in the future. She'd had so much faith back then, but look how it turned out. She admitted she felt betrayed by God.

I asked her if she ever told God how she felt. She said no.

"Just tell God. No agenda," I said. "Let God know how you feel and don't apologize. God can take it." *And if God can't*, I thought, *then God isn't God.*

Because, despite what the church often taught us, having dreams and desires, taking big risks, and feeling massive amounts of grief when it doesn't work out is just…human.

A couple weeks before Christmas, I resigned from a job at an abusive church. I was thirty-four years old, living on the West Coast. It had been about eight years since I left my family and the Christian patriarchy movement. I'd had prior church positions: one in the south, one in Mexico, one in the Midwest, and one on the East Coast. That West Coast church was my fifth and final church job, but I did not know that when I turned in my resignation.

For a couple months after leaving the church, I still attended other local churches and applied for other church positions. But after you see the toxic layers beneath the church system, you can't unsee it. I began to see the deeply embedded theological problems that lead to abuse in the evangelical church. I knew if I went back to working for the church, I'd end up in a similar situation—because it was everywhere.

Around the time I realized my career in the church was over, I visited a church where a friend was pastoring. I could not stop crying. It was a tiny church, meeting in an elementary school classroom, so I couldn't leave without my friend seeing me. I contained myself through the communion line, then I immediately fled to my car, my body having a visceral reaction. By then I understood trauma well enough to know my body was reacting to feeling unsafe.

I decided that was it. For the first time in nearly a decade, I was going to take a break from church.

I decided, for the first time in my entire life, I was going to take a break from God.

I always tried to be honest and vulnerable with God. I was a good Christian girl, and God already knew the thoughts of my heart.

But telling God I was pissed at them and then doing something about it (stopping church, stopping reading my Bible, and stopping talking to God altogether) was the most honest I'd ever been. I was angry at God. If God existed, they had betrayed me. Therefore, we were no longer on speaking terms.

A month later, the entire world shut down for the COVID pandemic. I'd already stopped going to church, and now almost everyone else had to stop, too.

I'd built my career around the church, and I was no longer going. I'd loved the Bible once, reading it nearly every day. But in the spring of 2020, all my various versions of the Bible were tucked away in boxes in my closet.

I used to pray all the time, constantly speaking to God. But as soon as I stopped, I felt I'd shed a massive burden. It felt like I'd rid myself of the final toxic connection to the church. I would eventually learn my relationship with God had been structured like an abusive one. And similar to most abusive relationships, you don't realize how extensive the damage is until you've packed your bags and fled to safety.

So many well-meaning people will tell survivors of spiritual abuse some equivalent of "That's not the real God. God wasn't the one who hurt you." But for many survivors, they cannot separate the actions of the church and the actions of God. This is not the survivor's fault. Most common theologies intricately connect the two.

For some survivors, making the separation is helpful. During my first round of recovery—after leaving my family system— I spent nearly a decade trying to figure out what was "real Christianity" and what was the lie.

The second round of recovery, nearly a decade later, when I was leaving the abusive West Coast church, the separation was no longer important. Both God and the church got put in the same box.

For what felt like the first time, I was free to explore all the questions the church had taught me to suppress. I was finally being extremely honest with God, admitting that I did not trust the God I'd grown up with and acknowledging maybe the God I thought I'd been serving did not actually exist.

Where will this journey end? I wondered. *Will it end with me deciding I'm no longer a Christian?* For the first time in my life, that did not scare me. I knew the friends and family who'd been a part of my life for decades would stop trusting me if I told them I wasn't a Christian (or even if they suspected it). I concluded this was a problem. If people only loved me because they thought I believed the same thing they did, then that wasn't a healthy relationship.

I had no idea the loss that would come in the next few years.

I also had no idea the freedom I'd find or the friendships I'd form, all from a willingness to acknowledge I was unhappy with the faith I had. All from a willingness to acknowledge I wanted more than the church and the God I believed in could give me.

My desire for freedom, for *more,* for better than what my faith had promised led me on the most intoxicating adventure yet.

From those early days when I first learned, at sixteen, that I would not be allowed to go to college, the quest for freedom caused me to look for cracks in the walls, for fissures in the foundation. Some part of me wanted more than the promises of this religious world I was living in, so I began looking. Cautiously. Secretly.

Beneath this quest was something I'd learned to fear—desire. Many of us on the other side of abusive religion explore the concept of desire, how systems that control human desires employ a highly effective method of controlling humans in general.

My friend Martha and I were texting about this recently. She said, "The untangling of that is so hard because ultimately in that culture it's be loved or follow your desires. That's the catch, right?

Conformity over authenticity—but you will be 'loved.' So of course we will squash our desires, because isolation is the ultimate hell."

You are only loved if you conform. You are only loved if you fit the prescribed ideal. If you dare to dream of something different, if you dare to choose your dream over the system's demands and expectations, you become an outcast.

How is this love?

It isn't. It's manipulation and coercion.

Yet how does someone escape this dynamic when the ones coercing conformity belong to your family? When they are your friends, your culture, your entire community?

How did I manage to take a big enough risk that things would be better if I followed what I wanted instead of adapting to my abusive environment? How did I manage to leave my family and risk homelessness? How did I manage to do the same thing again, nearly a decade later, when I left my job, my church, my community, and my chosen career?

I believe there was enough of a spark of hope, enough of a desire for something better, that was just strong enough for me to follow it and take the chance things *could* be better.

Desires are dangerous to high-control spaces. People who are tapped into their desires are alive and full of hope. It's difficult to control people who are fully alive. Forcing conformity is how these spaces keep people subdued—by conditioning people to surrender their desires to a God the power holders created to serve their own agenda.

THREE: COLLECTIBLES

We Were Just Trophies

MY PRECIOUS

Survivors often spend years wondering why they were the target of abuse. Was I too compliant? Too rebellious? Was I too pretty or not pretty enough? If I hadn't said this, would they have done that?

If I'd said no to the job…

If I'd decided not to move…

If I hadn't gone on that date…

One of my colleagues experienced sexual abuse from a babysitter for several years. After an encounter, the perpetrator would say, "This wouldn't be happening if you weren't so pretty." In her child's mind, this message took hold: Beauty leads to abuse. So, to prevent abuse in the future, she needed to avoid looking attractive. She spent the next two decades wearing baggy clothing in black and other muted colors. She avoided makeup and only gave her hair basic attention.

Often abusers convince us to blame ourselves because they actually believe a twisted tale. A perpetrator violates someone sexually because they believe they are entitled to the victim's body. A pastor controls a parishioner's spiritual life because they believe they alone know the will of God. A parent shames a child into submission because they believe the seemingly strong-willed child is bad and what's best for the child is to have their behavior curtailed.

The narrative the abuser tells their victim is one where the victim deserved the abuse. In the mind of many perpetrators, this narrative isn't just a story—it's reality, which is why it's so easy for the victim to internalize and believe it, even years upon years after the abuse has stopped.

Despite what we often hear in the media, abusers do not always go after the easy, discarded targets. While it's true that those who have been abused are at greater risk of being abused again, it isn't because of some flaw they inherently possess. Abusers, and a culture shaped by abusers, perpetuate this narrative—once again making the abuse the victim's fault, rather than the fault of the abuser.

As was the case with my colleague whose abuser blamed her beauty to justify his actions, abusers often pursue high-value targets. They like precious things. Shiny objects. They are Gollum, obsessed with the One Ring of Power.

PLEASE AND APPEASE

One of my favorite literary characters is Éowyn from *The Lord of the Rings*. Even as a teenager watching the films for the first time, I admired her scrappy determination, how she clawed her way to the life she wanted. And still got a cool romance with Faramir, someone who honored her strength—someone who wasn't afraid of her power.

As a family one evening, we were watching *The Return of the King*. My favorite scene arrived on the screen. Éowyn fights the Nazgûl king. The monstrous king mocks her, saying, "No man can kill me." Éowyn rips off her helmet. Her long blond hair flies free in the wind, revealing that she is not a male soldier but a woman. She declares, "I am no man"—then she stabs the king into dust.

I have always loved this scene, in both the film and the book. Yet it's attached to one very confusing memory.

After watching this scene as a family, my father turned toward the couch where my four sisters and I were jammed together. He beamed with pride. "She reminds me of my daughters."

I beamed back, delighted my father saw me in Éowyn, my fictional hero.

Decades later, I've had several therapists as part of my recovery from spiritual abuse. Each of my many therapists has described my patriarchal upbringing as confusing. This family viewing of *The Return of the King* is an example of that. My father was proud of our strength. Of our scrappy determination. Yet at the same time, he feared it and sought to suppress it.

The way I make sense of it now is my father didn't want us to be docile damsels in distress. He wanted us to be blunt weapons of power and grit. He just wanted those weapons in *his* hands so *he* could control them.

I have encountered a certain type of man a dozen times throughout my life. These controlling, patriarchal men like to collect competent people. They like to surround themselves with powerful people, with their own couchful of Éowyns. But *only* if they can control and manipulate those people.

Once you start fighting back, making your own choices, or, God forbid, thinking for yourself, they must douse your light and snuff out any inclination you might have to be a separate person.

This cycle rolled on repeat more times than I'm able to document during my time in my parents' home. We had to be excellent, write our letters perfectly inside the lines, and use my father's method for folding the dishrag to wipe down the counters. We had to show initiative to make my father happy and carry out whatever whim he felt important for the season. We had to represent our family and maintain the image of happiness and success.

But if we did something on our own, like watching a TV show without asking his permission or arriving at our own conclusion about something in scripture, he shamed us for defying his authority and doing what is right in our own eyes, using Judges 21:25 to frighten us away from having independent thoughts: "In those days there was no king in Israel; everyone did what was right in his own eyes."

Confusing, all my many therapists agreed. So very confusing.

Movies were often a point of contention in our family, as we had to get approval for anything my father hadn't seen yet. In my twenties, it felt so demeaning to ask my father's permission for movies, so I'd sneak them to forgo this rule, though the illicit viewing always ended with lingering anxiety he might find out.

A few times, he did find out. I never really knew how these things came about, and I really don't remember every instance of his discovery. I guess most of the time it was an accident. Either way, when he found out, it was never pleasant.

I borrowed the first three seasons of *Alias* from a friend who would later become my sister-in-law. I was in my early twenties. My friend's family was strict and conservative, so I figured if she was allowed to watch it, then it probably wasn't so bad.

I did not take into account that her parents didn't make her get permission for movies and shows when she was in her twenties, even though she also still lived at home with them.

My father discovered the DVDs of *Alias* and confronted me about them over ice cream on a father-daughter date night. His main critiques were about feminism and violence, but before he got too far in his tirade, I said, "Have you seen *Alias*? I think you'd like it. It's about a spy. Kind of like *Bourne Identity*."

Intrigued, my father tilted his head in a manner that said, "Tell me more." So, I told him the main storyline. I made sure that I mentioned the father-daughter relationship. Then, I don't really know why I said this, but I added, "It also shows the power a woman has with her body. Like, how it can be dangerous." I meant it as a positive thing. I mean, we had been told our whole lives we had the power to seduce men, so we needed to cover up. Then here was a show where a spy literally uses her body to gain power over men. The show confirmed what he'd always told me!

But my father's face sagged into disapproval, as if the power of seduction were never the point of all those modesty talks and admonitions to Save the Men by hiding your body.

Eventually, he watched *Alias* and enjoyed it like I predicted. It became a family show. Though I would have preferred to watch the DVDs by myself, it was a relief to not have to hide it anymore.

This same thing happened with a CD of music I compiled. My father discovered it when one of my sisters left it in the CD player of the car. That evening, he gathered the whole family around for a lesson in the evils of music.

However, as he went through each song, I countered his assessment, telling him about the good, wholesome things I experienced in each song. In the end, eight out of nine tracks received approval from Dad.

Though I won that round, I perfected my subterfuge by convincing my father that the contraband media was something that benefited him. I turned it into something he could enjoy and appreciate. I stroked his ego, demonstrating how he was right—that this music really did fit into his standard. I *was* listening to him and thinking about him when I made my media choices. He'd succeeded as a father. He'd taught me well, and I'd internalized his principles. He had been right the whole time, and the world really did revolve around him.

I suppose, in the end, I hadn't really won much of anything.

GASLIGHT

"Why did he think he could mess with me?" I said this a hundred times throughout my time working at the church on the West Coast. I was thirty-two when I took the job. It had been around six years since I left my family and the Christian patriarchy movement.

"He picked the wrong person to mess with" was a statement I said to my reflection in the mirror each time I needed motivation to keep going, to keep fighting for myself.

Bullies are cowards. I'd read this in an article about workplace bullies. Show strength, it said; the bully will eventually back down.

So, I showed strength. Each time my boss, Otis, sidelined me, silenced me, demeaned me, or said something false about me, I fought back. I called meetings with our department supervisor. I sent emails documenting encounters (and then saved those emails to an ever-growing file of evidence). For nearly a decade I'd done so much work surrounding my experience in my family of origin, I knew what I was seeing in Otis—another man who felt he was entitled to treat me any way he wanted because I was obligated (by employment terms and by the Bible) to be kind, and respectful, and extend grace. I was obligated to forgive and continue to want to work on our relational conflict. Those are the rules of a church job. Those are the rules of Christianity.

Otis knew those rules. So much so that he had most everyone convinced he was humble and wanted to work with me while portraying me as a disgruntled bitch who was never happy, no matter how hard he tried to please me. The first time he did this was the first time I went outside of our relational dynamic and went to Jean, the department director, for help. Her solution was to call a meeting.

The office was small, with four people taking up space in the same room. Jean, at least, was another woman in the room. She was an austere woman, cold and didn't smile much.

My internal radar was not picking up safety.

Alfred, my and Otis's direct supervisor, sat near her, his chair on Jean's side of the room. Alfred smiled a lot. I wished, in that moment, he wouldn't smile quite so much.

Otis wasn't smiling, but I noticed he'd made his tall, bulky frame small as he took a seat across from me. My inner radar picked up speed, registering danger before he even spoke.

Jean asked Otis to tell his side of the story. She'd already heard mine when I'd gone to her in tears the day before. We were leaving on a youth retreat that weekend, and she wanted this resolved before Otis and I were alone with teenagers.

Otis made himself even smaller. He spoke in a timid voice. "I spoke too harshly the other day, and I'm very sorry."

Jean asked me, "Do you accept Otis's apology?"

My inner radar whirred so wildly it was in danger of exploding. I looked back and forth between Jean and Otis, Alfred's grinning face between them.

Was that it?

They waited for my response as tears congested the back of my throat.

What the hell? What the fucking hell?

The word *gaslight* wasn't in my vocabulary at the time—but something of the form ping-ponged inside my brain. Gaslighting is when an abuser sets out to make their victim question their sense of reality. If they can discredit the witness by appearing calm (while deceiving their audience) in the face of their victim's emotional appeals, then most people will side with the abuser and write the victim off as unstable.

Right in front of me, Otis had lied. He penitently confessed to speaking too harshly when the real story was he'd berated me for two hours. He'd called me insubordinate, accused me of disrespect, and brought up incident after incident of things I'd done over the past six months, assigning the worst possible motives.

Harsh didn't even begin to describe it.

And because no one else was there to witness his tirade, I was caught in a vortex of he said, she said.

Jean blinked at me patiently. But the patient blinking hid what she wasn't saying.

She thinks I'm making this up.

The previous day I'd called an emergency meeting with her. I'd sobbed in her office, unsure what to do. I was aware I'd been triggered—too many of Otis's words resembled the words of my father. In my state of hyperarousal—an involuntary response to threat (real or perceived), usually a fight or flight response—I wasn't able to discern that he resembled my father because he was *like* my father.

I was still in a state of denial and couldn't fathom I'd moved across the country for this job only to have the same sort of man as a boss.

But there in that office, his description of "I spoke too harshly" was a dose of familiarity. I'd played a role in this scene a hundred times growing up, when my father would question my memory—when he'd say, "That's not how it happened" when I tried to communicate how his actions made me feel.

A deliberate questioning of my reality was happening in real time. And Alfred and Jean thought this would all go away as soon as I told Otis I forgave him.

I choked on tears, making a great effort to not cry in front of Otis. I could feel his contempt, though I was sure neither Alfred nor Jean could sense it.

My behavior was far from glamorous or badass, but I knew I couldn't just say "It's fine" and be done with it. I blubbered incoherently for several minutes, never fully accepting the apology nor admitting all was well. My mind was reeling, and I could sense Jean's patience ebbing away. Her face had grown stonier. She was ready for this mess to be done with.

Alfred continued grinning by her side, but his smile was slipping. Despite his optimism, he wasn't an idiot, and I think he knew this wouldn't be as clean and crisp as he'd hoped.

We all committed to discuss the situation again soon. After the retreat.

A couple weeks later, Jean announced she had taken another job—in another city. They would drop the case of Otis and Katherine—everyone preferring for it to just go away.

But the trembles of the earthquake had just begun.

MONKEYS

Several years after the experience with Otis, an abusive working relationship that lasted for nine months before he took another job, I interviewed Connie Baker on *Uncertain*, the Tears of Eden podcast that supports survivors of spiritual abuse from evangelical communities. Connie is a survivor of spiritual abuse and clergy sexual abuse. She is the author of one of the only practical books on the subject, *Traumatized by Religious Abuse,* and works as a therapist primarily with this demographic. She said she noticed a pattern with clients who had experienced chronic spiritual abuse in the church. Most of the time, these victims were highly competent, high-achieving individuals. They were rule-followers and cared about others.

Something clicked in my brain: why Otis had hired me in the first place when clearly he had a problem with my abilities, a point of tension that began to surface within my first few weeks of work.

My résumé was stellar. I had experience. I'd been introduced to the church of 1,500 members as an "expert" in youth ministry. I had a seminary degree, increasing the number of women on staff with this credential from one to two.

I made the church look good. I made the ministry look good. Otis managed to snag someone with my competence for the position, so my presence made him look good. I added to his appearance of success.

This all became so confusing when I realized he didn't actually want to be successful. If he had, he would have allowed an educated, experienced, and creative staff member to flourish and do what she did best. But he couldn't have this if he wanted to maintain control.

When he hired me, I believe he genuinely wanted me. But I think Otis thought he could control me. The micromanaging started within the first month of work. He turned one of the Sunday school classes over to me, saying things like "This will be your baby" and "You can make this your own. Do whatever you want." Yet he kept popping into the classroom, questioning what I was doing, critiquing.

Eight months later we were deep in the middle of a chaotic and toxic relational upheaval. The church leadership removed Otis from being my direct supervisor, but we were still running the youth ministry together. It was a Band-Aid prolonging a choice they didn't want to make. Eventually, they were going to have to choose between me and Otis.

One day I was talking to Alfred, the director of the family ministry and my new direct supervisor after Otis was removed from that role. We each held a glass mug of a latte we'd made from the espresso machine in his office and sat on the modern couch he'd purchased for his work space. "Otis knew what he was getting when he interviewed me," I said. "I was very honest about who I was. Nobody looks at my résumé and thinks 'administrative assistant.' I was very clear that I was an inventive leader. It's literally written at the top of my résumé. He *knew*, so why did he think he could treat me like his personal valet, tell me to take notes during our meetings, ask me to make copies for him, and basically require I turn off my brain?"

In one of the more comical moments of our season working together, Otis confronted me about the meeting notes I'd sent to the youth team. He showed me an example of what he wanted, which included everything in list form. "But you can decide how you want to do it," he said. "You can decide if you want to number the items or use bullet points."

Well, *thank you very much*. Thank you for confirming my ownership over the notes. I literally had full rein over my choices: bullet points or numbers.

I couldn't even take notes without his critique or supervision. He needed control of *everything*. Which constantly confused me as to why he'd hired *me* when what he wanted was a circus monkey who would jump through hoops in exchange for treats.

My interview with Connie Baker was the beginning of understanding why Otis hired me. I now know, after studying the dynamics of abuse for several years, that if abusers have a choice between success and control, they will choose control. They collect competent people and surround themselves with powerful people, but *only* if they have a way to control those people. The perfect tool in an abuser's hand is a highly skilled person who is eager to please.

What better place to find this sort of person than inside of a church where the culture trains people to be hardworking and codependent?

The most dangerous sort of person in the eyes of an abuser is someone who doesn't need them, who values their independence and self-respect more than the protection and approval of the abuser.

Otis underestimated me, and he eventually took a job at another church. But he still caused considerable damage. I didn't escape the war unscathed. To this day, when I make an assertive choice, I'll often experience a chill down my spine or a knot of foreboding in my gut—residual fear that I'm about to get in trouble for daring to think I can make a decision without consulting some male authority. This is just one small example of the subtle nature of spiritual abuse and the lingering trauma in the aftermath.

However, the worst damage came not from Otis but from the system that supported him and the culture of abuse it perpetuated.

FOUR: SYSTEM

Abusers Don't Work Alone

SYMPTOMS

Thirty-two staff left in the two years and three months I worked at the church. After a half dozen staff left, I started keeping count. As a joke, I made a *Game of Thrones*–style bracket to document who would be taken out next. When I finally left the church, I was number thirty-two.

At that church on the West Coast, I learned a lot. I had an opportunity to witness an abusive system with the resources of someone who'd been studying the dynamics of abuse for half a decade.

When I lived with my parents, our family system was all I knew. Figuring out what was right and what was wrong was so very complicated and confusing. I didn't have language for what was happening. I endured it until my mid-twenties, when I felt if I didn't change something, I would be miserable for the rest of my life.

At the West Coast church, I was older by several years. I'd lived in a couple different places and had a few different jobs. I'd been in therapy off and on for about four years. After working through a lot of what happened with my family, I had more language and more resources to name the abuse.

These resources and this language served me when I started seeing things at the West Coast church that didn't make sense—subtle and confusing inconsistencies.

A lot of upper-level tension—including confusion and conflict-ing narratives—existed at the church that trickled down to the lower-level employees. Some of the elders met with the staff to let us know they cared about us and were trying to fix things. A couple of the elders cried and apologized. I thought this was pretty amazing, as I'd never seen such public humility.

Then I looked around at some of my coworkers. Their faces were stone cold. As soon as that meeting was over, one of my coworkers said to me, "We've seen this before. They always cry and apologize, but nothing changes."

In the next few months, the church brought in therapists and trained mediators to try to address the issues. The leadership seemed really invested in fixing things. I participated in those mediation sessions with great enthusiasm. I was thrilled a church was actually addressing the problems—I'd never seen a church do this!

Then staff started leaving. They'd always be celebrated and sent off with great pomp and circumstance. But once the party ended, after the streamers were in the trash and the charcuterie was cleared away, I'd hear the real story from my coworkers. "He was pushed out," one told me after the farewell party for a pastor. "They don't fire you around here," one of my colleagues said. "They take away all your power until you are so miserable you leave on your own."

In the two years and three months I worked at that church, thirty-two staff left.

When we think of abuse, we often consider individual abusers and the impact they have on other individuals. However, I've learned abusers are rarely isolated in their abuse. For example, executive leadership enables, covers up, or assists the abusive pastor in their abuse; family members stay quiet about domestic violence; elders tell an emotionally battered wife she must submit to her husband.

Addressing one abuser rarely addresses the impact and connecting points of the system supporting that abuse.

In the last chapter, I talked about my experience with Otis. Once Otis left, I thought everything was going to be okay. Yet after about two months, I realized that the issues with Otis had distracted me from the issues in the wider church. Otis was a symptom of a toxic system.

He wasn't the only one. Nor was he working independently.

NARCISSISTS

It took a letter, with the stories and signatures of dozens of witnesses, to get the system to pay attention.

The denomination I worked for had an avenue for congregants to bring complaints about a pastor or ordained elder. If everyday church citizens felt like the ruling elders of the church were not adequately addressing a situation, the congregants could contact the higher-ups through a regional session. (The church government structure in this denomination functioned similarly to the U.S. government, containing local church sessions, regional sessions, and the highest tier, the general assembly for North America.) The process of complaint usually began with some sort of letter.

A woman who eventually became my friend organized witnesses to write a letter to the regional session in the Pacific Northwest. Dozens of current and former staff members, along with former elders and current and former congregants, included their testimonies and signed their names.

This letter set off an alarm, alerting the regional session that the situation was dire. An investigation ensued, and representatives began interviewing the witnesses, gathering credibility and evidence.

I did not sign the original letter, though I knew it existed. After I turned in my resignation, the committee conducting the investigation contacted me to hear my testimony.

Most of the abuse I experienced at the church came from Otis and the leadership assigned to help us, who were woefully under-trained in the dynamics of abuse or the indicators of trauma.

But as I've said, Otis was not an isolated appendage in this system. I didn't know the senior pastor very well, but I'd seen enough to know how pivotal he'd likely been in creating a culture that was attracted to narcissistic leaders. I had a handful of stories to share about this pastor, hopefully serving to corroborate the stories of dozens of other witnesses. I also hoped my story would dispel the narrative the church leadership was currently singing from their Sunday morning platform, the narrative that everything was better and everyone was happy.

I told the investigators several stories, most of them including the pastor's propensity to cross boundaries, such as disclosing personal information about others in contexts where it was inap-propriate, and exhibiting audacious behavior, such as usurping and derailing meetings. It was behavior no one else would get away with—and all potential symptoms of a narcissist.

Narcissistic personality disorder (NPD) is a diagnosable disorder in the *Diagnostic and Statistical Manual of Mental Disorders* (*DSM*). Though many narcissists in churches may very well have NPD, I am not diagnosing anyone here. Calling someone a narcissist is often an expressive term similar to calling someone an asshole. It might describe someone who wreaks havoc on the lives of others for their own gratification. For my purposes here, the narcissist is an abuser, someone in a position of power who uses that power to strip away the identity of their target. Many mental health profes-sionals cringe at using the word too loosely. I ascribe to the belief that a survivor gets to choose the word that best resonates with their circumstances. Many survivors of spiritual abuse in churches will instantly resonate with the description of a narcissist. So *narcissist* is the word I will use here.

This pastor would often do things that nobody else would ever dare to do. For example, in group staff meetings, I'd look around and wonder, *Did anyone else notice how he completely took over the meeting from the executive director?* But since everyone usually acted as if what was happening wasn't happening, I just stayed quiet.

Once, two staff members resigned around the same time. They were two more employees in an extended mass exodus of staff leaving the church. Another coworker and I organized a farewell party for the departing staff, who specifically requested no sadness. Just fun. No stories or sharing. Just laughter and food and drink.

We accommodated with a game show and wine and cheese.

As we gathered around the charcuterie board, laughing with glasses full of sparkling wine, this pastor suddenly drew all the attention to himself as he began sharing how much each of these two departing staff members meant to him (never mind that literally everyone in the room knew that they were leaving to get away from him and the toxic atmosphere of the church). Before he'd even finished the first paragraph of his speech, the pastor was weeping. Like, full-on-tears-streaming-down-his-face weeping.

I glanced furtively at my co-party-planner, wondering if we should do something. The two staff members had deliberately asked for fun and no sadness, yet here the pastor had commandeered the space and shifted the entire mood in one self-indulgent, rhetorical swoop. As I sat helplessly looking for a gap in the speech to perhaps insert some levity or shift the mood, it became so very obvious to me that the pastor wasn't there to celebrate the two employees, whom he called his "very dear friends;" he was there to express his feelings.

His speech was all about him, and that was exactly the way he wanted it.

He left the party immediately after this eulogy, and we all returned to fun and games, perhaps with a bit more enthusiasm to wash away the awkwardness. It was around this time that I realized I was absolutely over this pastor. I felt like what he'd done was entirely selfish, and I wanted to apologize to my soon-to-be-ex-coworkers on his behalf.

That's another symptom of a relationship with a narcissist: Somehow, they manage to make you feel responsible for their boundary-crossing and audacious behavior. We all do awkward things. We all commit social faux pas. The difference between most people and a narcissist is the narcissist always shifts the blame for their behavior to someone else—even if this shifting is ever so subtle.

One or two instances may not be enough to call foul. But over time, a narcissist will reveal themselves in a pattern of audacious behavior and crossing boundaries. Watch. Listen. Observe. They will reveal themselves before long.

After sharing this story with the elders investigating the claims in the original letter of complaint, along with a few other examples, I took the opportunity to communicate that I didn't think removing the senior pastor would address the problem. While I believed he was too unhealthy to be a pastor, I also didn't think he was the primary issue.

"The issue is in the system," I said. "The system is designed by a narcissist, and that design requires a narcissist to maintain. If you get rid of him, a new narcissist will be leading the church very soon." I genuinely believed my prophesy, but even I didn't know the new narcissist was already at the church: the executive director the church had recently hired. This director stepped into the void left behind when the regional session for our denomination eventually removed the senior pastor from his position.

Long after I left, I heard story after story of this director's audacious behavior, including mistreatment of staff, as well as overt racism, sexism, and misogyny.

Abusers need the abusive system to survive. If an abuser gets into a position of power, it's imperative you address the system that put them there, including, but not limited to, the internalized system within yourself. If you don't, you'll end up right back in the same situation. Different players, but the same dynamics.

STRANGE RULES

The evangelical church has strange rules. For example, it often has an aversion to things like smoking, drinking, cussing, and dancing too much with your booty (or dancing at all). This is especially true if the church is located in what is known as the Bible Belt. However, conservative culture exists all over the country and all over the world. From a very young age, I found these rules confusing. I once asked Nana, "Why is it bad to cuss?" She responded, "Because bad people cuss."

Bad people made cussing bad.

The logic being if bad people cuss, then cussing will make you look like a bad person.

I think.

A few years ago, I was visiting Nana. I got a phone call from a friend and went outside on the porch to talk.

I must have said a few f-words during the conversation (not uncommon for me), because when I came back inside, Nana asked me if I was still a Christian.

This question seemed to come out of nowhere. "What do you mean?"

"Because you use such foul language," she clarified.

I probably shouldn't tell her that I own multiple vibrators and a healthy amount of lube.

While these rules exist in wider church culture, the renegades within always seem to find one another.

Just after obtaining my college degree, about a year before I left the South to move to Mexico for a year (to work at the church plant where I wasn't invited to the planning meetings), I was on a women's beach trip. The church I attended at the time had disbanded affinity groups, meaning they combined all adult Sunday school groups and no longer relegated the singles ministry into a glorified youth group of adults waiting in an incubator until we had ripened fully enough to enter the season of marriage.

This meant they no longer had a focused women's ministry, so the beach trip was unofficially sanctioned by the church. There were no speakers or organized events, just a bunch of women renting beach houses and drinking a lot of wine.

In the churches I attended as an adult, wine was always in a different category than cocktails or liquor. Wine and beer were socially acceptable at most events.

Like I said, the church has strange rules.

Only a handful of the women on this retreat were husbandless and childless. We single women all got assigned to the same house. One woman in this house was married with children, but she didn't wear frumpy clothes or have a thick fringe hairstyle. She wore two-piece bathing suits, so I guess they assigned her to our house because they thought she'd be more comfortable with us than with the other moms.

She was very cool and became our gang leader. We unofficially elected her because she was married with children and therefore more mature and more equipped to lead us.

On the final night of the beach trip, she led us down the decadent path of booze and cigarettes. Each beach house came with a couple of bikes. So, late in the evening, we mounted up and rode from house to house, making calls upon our fellow retreat attendees.

We found one of our members making a contraband pitcher of margaritas. We convinced her and her pitcher to join us, filling our disposable cups with margaritas and definitely riding while under the influence.

Our married leader took us far away from the houses of the other women, seeking out a secluded park bench before she pulled out her pack of cigarettes and passed them around.

A couple years before this, another church friend had taught me how to smoke, and I was glad this wasn't my first time. I really wanted these women to think I was cool.

We rode our bikes around and around, howling at the moon, ducking behind bushes when we saw one of the other church ladies. Our married leader made us put our cigarette butts in an empty cup (because all good leaders care about the environment). We may have been heathens, but we did not litter.

After this beach trip, a couple of these women became my actual friends. I started volunteering with the youth ministry, and smoking and drinking after

Wednesday night youth group became a regular occurrence.

We always sat on the back porch of one of our houses, porch lights off in case someone from the church drove by and recognized us.

After I left ministry as a vocation, I left institutional religion as well. While I don't miss most things associated with organized religion (mainly, all the strange rules), I do miss the community these institutions often provide. I miss the camaraderie surrounding a cigarette and a beer on a Wednesday night.

Few places exist that allow community to develop in an organic way. The church does it so well.

Except you have to follow the strange rules to be a part of it.

Or be really good at pretending.

SECOND-WAVE FUNDAMENTALISM

At the time I entered the public scene to educate people about the impact of spiritual abuse, circa 2020, hundreds of folks were online talking about faith deconstruction. For context, faith deconstruction post evangelicalism is a common phenomenon that occurs when someone finds their faith practice lacking for any number of reasons.

Perhaps they saw the way the church treated the queer community and left because they were appalled at the hatred and shame they saw inside congregations that professed to be loving.

Perhaps they'd been abused by a pastor and experienced more abuse when they'd tried to get help from the church leadership.

Maybe they just saw inconsistencies everywhere and finally decided they could no longer deal with the hypocrisy.

Whatever the reason, deconstruction-focused podcasts, Instagram accounts, TikTok videos, and chatroom feeds surfaced everywhere. Some of these folks had thousands of followers. They were trying to address what was wrong with the church, most attempting to create a new path. "That isn't real Christianity," they'd say. "*This* is real Christianity."

In the early days of *Uncertain* and its Instagram account, I connected with a handful of other podcasters. We collaborated on episodes, had a group chat, and supported each other's content.

Within a year, four out of six of us were no longer podcasting. They disappeared from the public scene, content going cold. I observed the wider deconstruction world as one content creator after another announced they were taking an indefinite hiatus. Some announced they were no longer Christian and wanted to take a break from anything to do with Christianity. Some needed to care for their mental health. Others disappeared without giving a reason. Many burned out after exploding onto the scene, gaining a massive following and then…nothing.

As the following for *Uncertain* grew slowly, I watched, curious if one day I'd join the ranks of those who needed to move on. I suspected some of the burnout came after a creator's content grew so rapidly they didn't have the opportunity to create boundaries to protect their health. They posted every day, responded to direct messages within an hour, and gained hundreds of new followers every week.

Another pattern emerged, one that concerned me more than the burnout—I watched as the communities that formed in the deconstruction world appeared to mirror the same communities we left. Leaders prescribed what was right and what was wrong. They told us who to follow and who to cancel. Leaders who used to be pastors in the institutional church were now pastoring through social media—breaking down the scriptures to tell us what these verses *really* meant. They told us who was in and who was out. They became the new gatekeepers.

At some point, I started using the term *second-wave fundamentalism* to describe those of us who left high-control comunities only to recreate those same communities in spaces we had initially formed to be healthy. I watched as pastors who'd been abused in their congregations went on to form new, safe churches to reach those who'd been wounded. Then, those same pastors who'd been abused turned around and abused their congregants.

Male pastors who'd once been a part of a system dominated by men tried to create equitable systems by placing women in leadership. Then we'd discover a dark side to the pastors' motives, as they surrounded themselves with women as a new way to maintain power and control. Some women were so grateful for the opportunity they overlooked red flags. If any of those women pushed back, or became more influential than the pastor, the pastor's ego would flare, revealing their inclusive actions were just a smoke screen to hide their quest for power.

I saw abusive people rise to places of influence by creating a platform around advocacy for survivors of abuse. I knew abusers who were headlined at conferences for their remarkable work fighting for justice, mesmerizing audiences with their dynamic preaching, while leaving a trail of victims in their wake.

These patterns left me disheartened, and I sought out friends and colleagues to search for some sort of clarity on what was happening. I invited my colleague Laura Anderson, cofounder of the Religious Trauma Institute and founder of the Center for Trauma Resolution and Recovery, onto the podcast to address this second-wave fundamentalism, and her insight helped shore up some of the confusion. We discussed how in Christian fundamentalist spaces we approached life and beliefs through our cognition. Belief systems are cerebral. However, Laura said, "But simply untangling beliefs does not necessarily untangle how those beliefs have lived and functioned in your body."

Our minds are not separate from our bodies. Our minds are our bodies. They are intricately connected.

Laura explained, "When messages come in over time, whether it's repeated messages or overwhelming messages and experiences, they create what we call neural pathways in our brain. And then those neural pathways create chemicals and send them down to our bodies."

We can't avoid the influence cognitive beliefs have on our bodies' memories. We cannot simply change our beliefs by deciding we no longer believe something, especially if that system is embedded into our neural network.

As an example: Cognitively, I was so tired of listening to straight white men. I'd had enough of their bravado and authoritative teaching. Yet if a white man said something confidently, I found myself believing him almost instantly. Even when I was aware of this tendency, I still got sucked in, because I'd been conditioned by the systems I grew up in to trust white men and see them as symbols of authority—even when they had done nothing at all to earn my trust. In the patriarchal family and church systems I was raised in, men were God's chosen leaders.

I had to take serious steps to create new neural pathways. I stopped listening to podcasts led by white men. I stopped reading their books. I only invited a straight white man on my podcast every once in a while.

And I discovered I did not miss anything. In fact, I gained access to incredible, beautiful wisdom. There are women, queer people, and people of color doing amazing work. Often, they are doing better work, with higher quality and greater depth. I started to wonder how white men ever achieved so much power in the world. The wealth of wisdom in the wider world is so incredibly vast. How did this one demographic of people become so overwhelmingly influential?

The answer is in the neural network. We have been conditioned by our caregivers, our teachers, our communities, and our wider society to see a certain demographic of people as trustworthy, powerful, and ideal. Those messages are ingrained in our marrow. When entire groups of people with the same neural conditioning gather together, a system is formed. Simply declaring we no longer believe something cannot alter centuries of systemic conditioning.

Addressing the cognitive belief is important. But we mustn't stop there. We must also address the embedded network of beliefs that have formed pathways in our nervous system.

FIVE: LEAVING

The Brave Choice

NARRATIVES

When people leave the church, pastors and leadership will often perpetuate the narrative that the person left for any number of reasons: They were weak. They were lukewarm. Their faith wasn't grounded in truth. They weren't interested in real biblical teaching. True believers stay. True believers love God and the church so much they will never give up.

I previously mentioned that when I worked at the West Coast church, thirty-one staff members left before I did. This mass exodus occurred over the course of two years and three months. Some staff were let go, but most left of their own volition, taking a new job or quitting without a safety net.

Yet I watched as church leadership told one story to the congregation and one story to the staff. The story they told the congregation was that the person who left got a new, exciting opportunity. We're so happy for them!

The story they told the staff was that folks left because they couldn't hack it. They gave up when the going got difficult.

I knew both of these stories were a lie. Most of the folks who left had become my friends in the short time I worked with them. I knew how much they struggled. I knew how much they tried to make it work. I witnessed them begging the leadership for change.

I read the letters they sent to the elders. I stayed up late at night with them, talking and talking and talking.

They left because they felt like they had no other choice. Sometimes, they'd been pushed to the brink of their sanity. Sometimes, they felt in danger—their family wasn't emotionally or spiritually safe. They were exhausted from fighting. Their mental health was so depleted they could barely function.

My last six months at the church, I thought I was experiencing a bout of allergies when I started throwing up every morning before I even had any food in my stomach. I started getting migraines nearly every day. Gratefully, my doctor approved three weeks of medical leave, and that extra time off was the only reason I didn't have an emotional breakdown. I made it another month before I resigned.

Several weeks after I left, the morning vomit sessions stopped. So did the headaches. The stress of the work environment had taken a physical toll on my body. I didn't leave the church because I was weak or lacking faith. In fact, I would say leaving is often the stronger choice. The risky choice.

It's the choice nobody wants to make.

I remember finding out in my late teens that the wife in a family we'd known all my life had left her husband and seven children. She moved to a different city. I remember the adults whispering that she'd gone crazy. I remember they said she left because she wanted to wear bikinis—this little detail suggesting she left because she was selfish.

I now wonder what sort of misery this woman experienced to be willing to leave her children behind. Maybe she finally had a breakdown. Maybe caring for seven children became too much. Maybe the rules of the church and the community were more than any person could handle without falling to pieces. I know enough about the narratives people whisper about lost sheep to know she might have left to preserve her sanity—not because she lost it.

When I left the West Coast church, it took about six months from the moment I knew I needed to leave to the moment I actually left. This, in my opinion and experience, is quite fast. Most of the time it takes years of wrestling, weighing the cost, trying to make it work. It takes years of planning.

I believe my departure beat the average because I'd done the leaving once before. Many years prior to the West Coast church, I left my family.

RUN

We were a family of runners. While we all dabbled in other sports, running was one we all did together. They featured us in our city newspaper. A full headline spread of us in our athletic attire, two parents and seven children, all smiling faces, as we ran together toward the finish line.

The photo was taken in our driveway. It was a quarter-mile long, and we'd use it for sprint and interval training. Whenever I'd train by myself, I'd always stop just before the driveway sloped up into a hill. That hill was steep. It led to the house with beige siding, hidden by untamed hydrangea bushes that always attracted so many carpenter bees.

Whenever I trained with my siblings, I'd always run the hill. Because they ran the hill, and nothing is more motivating than sibling competition.

I probably ran that driveway a thousand times for exercise.

But I never imagined one day I'd run it to get away.

I actually don't know why I ran down the driveway that night. Walking would have achieved the same result. Was I afraid my father would come after me? Change his mind?

I ran, bags banging against my rib cage, full of the belongings I'd hastily shoved into them. Once I reached the end, I stood huffing with my bags grasped in my arms, anxiety swirling until I saw the headlights of Naomi's car. It was winter, but I don't remember the cold. I only remember wanting to get away as fast as I could.

Naomi had been waiting for my call. I think she'd been waiting for years. On one of the many nights I went to her, sobbing and conflicted, she'd led me through her kitchen to a small room near the laundry. "This bed is for you if you ever need it," she said, indicating a cot with white sheets. Naomi is eight years older than me. Her father disowned her when she was a teenager. For this, she teetered on the edge of being a dangerous friend, because she had no male authority in her life.

The night I ran down the driveway, she answered after two rings. "He told me to get out," I said.

"I'm on my way," she responded.

I then packed like a tornado was coming, getting to shelter before the worst of the storm came, taking only essentials.

I don't know why I ran down the driveway, though. What more could he do? He'd called in the ultimate price. The thing I'd always feared had happened. He'd finally done his worst—kicking me out of the house.

Naomi drove me to my grandmother's, which felt less intrusive than imposing on my friend. I was in shock and laughed nervously as I carried my stuff into Nana's. *What am I going to do? What did I just do?*

Naomi stayed with me for hours.

That night, and over the next few weeks, I kept saying the mantra in my head, *I'm nearly twenty-five years old. I should not have to ask my dad for permission to take a job.* I kept saying it over and over, grasping this small piece of logic for the lifeline it was.

Ever since the previous summer, when my father tried to coerce an apology from me and I stood my ground for two weeks before compromising with a small lie just to appease him, I knew the number one thing I needed to prevent this situation from happening again was money.

Naomi had gotten me a part-time job working for a church in her neighborhood. I started working while my father was out of town and informed him I'd taken the job after I'd already been working for three weeks.

Just after dinner, while my siblings cleaned up the kitchen and my mother was far away in another area of the house, I made my confession in the center of the dining room. Almost too quickly he responded, "Quit the job. Immediately." He didn't say anything else, leaving his unspoken "You knew what I'd say if you did something like this. Now you're reaping the consequences" to settle on us as I walked away without committing to follow through. Looking back, he likely thought it was a done deal. I'd never in my life defied a direct order.

I'm nearly twenty-five years old. I should not have to ask my dad for permission to take a job.

The one hurdle I knew might present a barrier to this uncertain plan of mine was the fact that he owned the cars. But I'd concluded the reason I didn't have my own was because he hadn't allowed us to have too much money. If we made money, it had to be in a prescribed way that fit his idea of an acceptable career for a woman. There were very few jobs like this that appealed to me.

I'd been considering a vocation in ministry for a few years, so taking a job at a church seemed like an appropriate step. I also just wanted the job.

All of these arguments might have been acceptable in my father's eyes if I'd deigned to ask his permission prior to starting the job. But I was tired of the anxiety associated with placing my future in his hands every time I wanted to make a change in my life.

I knew full well what could happen. I'd lived with the man my whole life.

I'm nearly twenty-five years old. I should not have to ask my dad for permission to take a job.

The day after he told me to quit, I went to work as usual. I came home as usual. The minute my father got home he asked me, "Did you quit the job?"

"No," I said simply.

"Why not?" he asked.

"Because I don't think it's wrong."

Oh, how many hours of anxiety and rehearsal went into saying those words. The words of subterfuge, of declaring my autonomy, of becoming the sort of woman my father feared and hated: an independent one.

He sighed. "Okay then. Get out." He said the words like I'd forced his hand. Like it was *me* who was coercing *him*.

I made no reply and went upstairs to pack.

It's funny how unsurprised I was, because he'd never threatened to kick any of us out. As we got older, he got more creative with his punishments, withholding money or material possessions or favor.

Kicking a child out of the house was extreme, even for him. And that's why I think I ran down the driveway.

My father did not expect me to defy him, to hold out once he pronounced my fate. He expected me to come back and say I was sorry and beg him to let me stay.

When I didn't behave as expected, there was a part of me that feared he would change his mind, realizing the consequence was too harsh. And that part of me was worried he'd try to bargain with me, and because I was so terrified, I thought I might give in.

I guess I do know why I ran down the driveway. I wasn't running away from *him*. I was running from my tendency to comply.

NEGOTIATIONS

I sat on the vibrant spring grass while my father berated me, but I don't remember his words. I only remember the green grass and the ducks who waddled along the edge of the city park pond. Waddled and waddled and plopped in the water, unaware of and unconcerned about the conversation (monologue) taking place just above them on the manicured park lawn.

After he kicked me out of his house, I lived in Nana's spare room and borrowed a car from the church where I worked, the part-time job I refused to quit. After a few days, when I still had not apologized, quit my job, or begged to return home, my parents entered into negotiations with me.

It was the first time in my life I had any leverage, because I realized my father hadn't expected me to hold out for so long.

He told my younger siblings they weren't allowed to go to Nana's as long as I was living there. Punishing Nana, too, for giving me shelter. For whatever reason, he did not extend the mandate to Joann and Macey, my two sisters just younger than me, telling them they could make their own decision about me, though he applied enough pressure that their interactions with me were kept secret.

Despite the chaos, when my twenty-fifth birthday arrived, I actually enjoyed my birthday party. A few friends from church, and Joann and Macey, came to celebrate me at a local, family-owned Mexican restaurant. I had fun. It might have been the first celebration I'd ever had where my parents were not involved in any way.

Oh, so I can celebrate my own birthday without them? This was a new experience.

I liked it.

Negotiations started a couple days after I left. We had a snowstorm. The South doesn't have the equipment to manage ice on the roads, as it occurs so infrequently. I had no experience driving on icy roads, so when I slid on ice and rear-ended an SUV in a borrowed car, I thought God might be punishing me.

But no, I couldn't believe God would want me to obey my father in this. If God was really a God of love and grace, he wouldn't be this vindictive. God was not my father. God was not an egomaniac who needed to control his children.

But that didn't stop the barbs of shame that followed an email from my mother, telling me the car accident was a sign the Lord was trying to teach me something. If I could have filed an insurance claim without their knowledge, I would have.

Okay, so maybe God didn't cause the car accident to punish me, but wasn't I dealing with enough? Could he have at least prevented it?

For a couple weeks, my father demanded to meet with me and I continued to counter with an offer to meet with a mediator. Finally, my father said he wouldn't meet with a mediator until I met with him first. While I had no desire to meet with him alone, my father wasn't known to outright lie or overtly renege on a promise. So, I agreed to a meeting in a park. An open space with people walking by, so maybe the location would put a cap on how many decibels his voice would reach.

I don't remember his words, but I remember his face. Eyes wide, brow creased, jaw tense.

Rage.

The topic of negotiations during those weeks expanded beyond whether I would quit the job or not. I finally had an opportunity to express how I felt. Maybe under these circumstances, my father would hear me.

The mediator of choice was the father of my best friend, Anne. We both lived at home in our mid-twenties, only she had been allowed to go to college. Her father had a similar worldview to my father's, and I knew my father respected him (if he respected anyone). If anyone could get through to my father, it would be this man because he had similar family values.

Anne's father had the idea that when my parents arrived at his home, I would share my piece, then I would leave so he could talk to my parents alone. I'd told Anne's father about the suicide attempt of one my sisters, and I think this got his attention in a way my getting kicked out of the house did not.

My parents entered and we all sat down in the living room. They had ornate furniture with leather couches and rugs that reminded me of something I imagined would come out of an estate in India.

I shared, very tentatively, how I was feeling. I avoided inflammatory words like *suffocation* and *trapped*. I focused more on how I just wanted to be treated like the adult I was. When I was finished, I got up to leave.

My mother tried to stop my flight. "We haven't discussed the main reason we are here: Katherine's rebellion."

Anne's father said, "Katherine can stay if she wants to."

I didn't want to, so I left.

Only later did I realize my mother hadn't heard a single word I said. My parents were zealous in their purpose for negotiating: corral an errant daughter before she got too far away.

I don't know the ins and outs of what happened that night. I only remember my mother telling me later that Anne's father had berated my father.

I wish I could have been a fly on the wall, even though this description was likely inaccurate. I'd had too many interactions with my father to know he often saw disrespect where none existed.

As part of the negotiations, my father and Anne's father met alone a few times. After one of these father meetings, Anne's father told me my father had brought up my writing—an interest of mine since childhood—as an example of my rebellion. I don't remember writing being a point of contention between my father and me, so the fact that he raised the issue confused me. We rarely talked about my writing. *I* rarely talked about my writing. Not to him. Writing was too precious to subject to his scrutiny.

Either way, I remember Anne's father growing very sad. He glanced away from me and said, "I just feel like—if my daughter told me she wanted to be a writer—I feel like I'd do everything I could to help her be a writer."

The words left me feeling numb, but over two decades later, I remember the contrast between fathers. I remember intellectually noting that good fathers support their children's dreams. I remember allowing myself to wonder if—perhaps—my father was not a good father.

Negotiations lasted eight weeks. My parents and I reached an agreement near the end of April. I remember being clear that I would only move back in with my parents if three conditions were met:

1. They did not ask me to apologize.
2. They admitted they played a role in creating this situation.
3. They invited me back home. No demands.

I did not communicate my conditions to my parents, yet they met every requirement. Though my father didn't take any responsibility, my mother said, "We don't know how to have an adult daughter. We are still learning." She used my word: *adult*. Maybe, just maybe, I'd gotten through.

It was good enough. I moved back in with them a couple days later.

Again in my old room, with my bed and furniture just the way I'd left it, I knew I'd made the right choice for the time being. I only had a part-time job. I hadn't started college yet. I didn't own a car. I didn't have a savings account.

My first night in my room, Macey crawled into bed with me. Her body snuggled up beside me told me she was glad I was home. But then the tears started coming, hot and violent and full of despair. I tried to muffle my sobs so I wouldn't disturb Macey. I don't know what I wanted. I don't even know why I cried. But I continued to cry until I fell into a fitful sleep.

SUFFER

The narrative that we leave because we gave up couldn't be more false. For someone experiencing domestic violence, there are massive financial, emotional, and psychological reasons for staying and staying and staying—oh so much longer than you want to.

Layer on top of this the additional compulsions instigated by the authority of God. I often say my father was a genius at mind control when he got me to fear God and believe God wanted me to obey my father. My father didn't invent this form of body snatching. Every cult leader employs some version of this. What made my situation that much more difficult was the culture of Christianity we all lived in. In the South where I grew up, most people have a reverence for God and the church, even if they don't actively participate in Christian traditions.

While some everyday Christians may have thought my family was strange when the daughters weren't allowed to go to college and when every child living at home spent all day every Saturday engaging in physical labor to build my father's mansion, it wasn't considered abuse.

So many experiences fall in the realm of emotional, psychological, and spiritual abuse, but we just think it's Christianity.

Layer on top of *that* all the admonitions in Christianity that orient us toward praising God in our suffering. I heard the story many times about how the apostles of Christ rejoiced when they were persecuted: "And after calling the apostles in, they flogged them and ordered them not to speak in the name of Jesus, and then released them. So they went on their way from the presence of the Council, rejoicing that they had been considered worthy to suffer shame for His name" (Acts 5:40–41).

Oh, how many women in abusive marriages have been counseled to return home to their abuser and suffer for Christ that they might win their husbands to the Lord. I am a legacy of this teaching. My father's mother likely died for this teaching. I believe my mother is still trapped because of it.

The way this teaching is often used in Christianity is coercive and manipulative. It's spiritual abuse. When someone is shamed for taking themselves to safety, it's abuse. Such teaching elevates the abuser's "good" above the other. (But we won't ever call the other a victim, because that would be admitting abuse exists.) This is a massive power differential.

I believe the reason why so many of us survivors write, why we tell our stories in books, online, and on podcasts, is because of the narratives around our departure. We were damned no matter what choice we made. If we stayed, we were oppressed to the point of mental and physical illness—sometimes death. If we left, we were erased and our story was told on our behalf by the ones who abused and neglected us, portraying us as the rebellious renegades who gave up their values and their faith out of selfish desires.

So, we tell our stories to reclaim the narrative. If for no one else, we tell it for ourselves, to remind us every day how much we lost and how much we suffered.

We tell our stories to celebrate the freedom we won at the cost of our literal blood, sweat, and tears.

We tell our stories to help others get to freedom.

We tell our stories so we won't ever go back.

KATHERINE SPEARING | 77

PIVOTAL

A narrative about those eight weeks of negotiations with my parents circulated not long after I returned to their home. One family friend said my father told him he let me move back home after I apologized. I don't know if this is really the story my father shared, but if he did, he likely believed it, though I was there and remember being very clear that I would not move home if it required I apologize. I was clear from the very beginning: *I am nearly twenty-five years old. I should not have to ask my dad for permission to take a job.*

I moved back home, and while it felt like regression, my father and I ceased talking about anything substantial. It was a relief.

Those first few months with me back in his home, my father was all niceness and charm. He loaned me money to buy a car. I made sure the car was registered in my name only. I also went to the bank and removed both of my parents from having access to my bank account. Whether I paid him back or not, that car was mine from the day I signed the papers with my own name.

But I paid him back. Every penny. I couldn't pay the money back fast enough.

In addition to the part-time job at the church that I did not quit, I got a job working as a nanny. I started taking college-level placement exams to pursue the illicit college degree—single-minded in my determination to secure everything I needed to be independent from my parents before I left them for good.

In the interlude where I was in negotiations with my parents, one pivotal moment permanently flipped the switch in my mind.

One of the pastors at the church I worked for had heard about what happened. I don't know how he knew my parents or heard about things without me telling him. Maybe he didn't know them at all—he just saw the signs and recognized them for what they were. He came into my office on the third day after I'd been kicked out.

I froze when he closed the door.

"The average abused woman leaves seven times before she leaves for good." After saying these words, he turned around, opened the door, and left.

This was the first time *anyone* had ever named my experience as abuse.

The pastor also provided me with a statistic I was determined to beat. Even three days into the separation, I knew I'd end up going back to live with my parents. I didn't have the resources to survive on my own. But I determined the next time I left, I'd make sure I had everything I needed so I would never, ever go back.

ESCAPE

Many of the staff who left the church on the West Coast also moved to different cities and different states. One survivor told me they weren't thrilled about their new job; they just had to get away. They uprooted their entire family to create distance. This doesn't strike me as the action of someone who "couldn't hack it" or someone who just gave up. It rings of desperation, the sort of desperation someone escaping a hostile regime might experience.

Working for a church isn't just a job. It's a lifestyle. Your work touches every area of your life. You have to be intentional about creating alternate universes, with separate hobbies and communities that aren't connected to the church. Your colleagues aren't just your coworkers. They're your friends and sometimes your family. You're connected to other churches in the denomination by layers of just one or two acquaintances. The senior pastors almost always know each other—even in different countries. If you haven't heard of a church in the denomination, odds are high one of your immediate colleagues has.

Taking a new job in a different city or a different state is extremely disruptive. I've embarked on this journey several times. While I was solo each time, and this held its own complications, I can't imagine the trauma associated with moving yourself, your partner, and your children.

When I moved to the West Coast, one member of the congregation at the church I was leaving made a validating statement: "Moving to a new city is as traumatic as losing a loved one." Hearing this caused me to exhale a good bit of tension from my body, as I recognized each transition, from one city to the next, as the traumatic experience it actually was.

When I moved from the East Coast to the West Coast, I was moving for the fifth time, to my fifth church job. I was finally able to give myself some compassion for going a little bit crazy for a few months after each move. I even started telling new coworkers that I wasn't myself and that I needed a few months to settle in—just so I wouldn't make enemies when I was withdrawn or if I randomly burst into tears.

Of course moving can be as traumatic as losing a loved one. You actually lose loved ones when you leave. Maybe they haven't died, but you lose the privilege of having them in your life every day. You are uprooted from the spaces and surroundings that have become your home. You must learn to navigate a new city, find out where the grocery store is, and figure out your preferred route to the office. You must find a new doctor, dentist, and optometrist. You have to set up a new bank account and find a trustworthy auto mechanic.

Moving to a new city is even more difficult when you're moving to get away from something, rather than moving to gain something—like a dream job or closer proximity to family. Just think of how difficult circumstances have to be for someone to go through this process to get away from a church. Sometimes, leaving an abusive church is as difficult as leaving an abusive family. You don't know if life on the other side will be better, you just know you can't stay any longer.

So, you strategize. You plan. You lie. You hide. You say you're going to a funeral when you're really going to a job interview. You get a separate personal cell phone because your work phone is on the church plan and they might see your calls and text records. You save emails that might help you out if you're wrongfully terminated. You have a list of safe people you can talk to, but those people are often on the church leadership's bad list. You avoid posting photos with them on social media. You meet in each other's homes so you won't accidentally be spotted together in public. You call ahead to see who will be at weddings or birthday parties so you won't risk running into a dangerous pastor or one of their henchmen.

Maybe nobody is going to physically harm you, but you know you are not safe. You're on high alert. Always.

Eventually, for whatever reason becomes that proverbial last straw, you decide it is time to go. You just can't live like this anymore, because it isn't living. It's survival. And our bodies can only function in survival mode for so long before they start breaking down.

Despite all of this, we can't control the narrative the power holders will spin once we've gotten away. I've heard from a few sources that my parents tell their acquaintances they are more than willing to meet with their children to try to reconcile. "Our children won't talk to us," they say. "We'll do whatever we need to do. We'll meet whenever and wherever they want."

What they *don't* say is that we have tried all that. Dozens of times. My siblings have also moved away and have their own stories to share. We have all written them letters. We've all tried meeting with them alone, with mediators, and with counselors. Our stories do not satisfy my parents, who appear to have decided our reasons for not trusting them—and for some of us, our reasons for separating completely—aren't good enough. They posture that our response is extreme for hurt feelings. *Abuse? What a laugh! We gave our children everything. A warm house, food, braces, and expensive vacations.*

Abuse? Show me the bruises. Show me broken bones.

There aren't any. Spiritual abuse doesn't work like that.

SIX: COLLATERAL DAMAGE

The People We Leave Behind

COMPLEXITY

How do you describe the complexity of a relationship with someone you love and care for who you believe is also an abuser? For
survivors, this relationship is often more excruciating than a relationship with a person who is an obvious villain.

With my father, it's simpler. I have no memory of affection for
my father. All interactions throughout childhood, teenhood, and
adulthood comprise walking around with tightly wound insides,
keeping it together for just a few more minutes.

Compliance never joy, excitement, expectation, or hope.

With my mother, the memories swirl with morning sunrises
and warmth. Some of it's true. Some of it, I believe, came from
a survival mechanism. I just couldn't fathom I had two unsafe
parents, so my survival brain created one villain and one victim.
And for most of my life, that's how I saw my mother: as a fellow
victim.

In abusive systems, abusers we care about are often abused. This
leads to a complex dynamic. You want to help them. You believe,
if you say the just-right thing, they will wake up like you did.
Then one day you realize if you keep trying to save them, you will
continue to put yourself in danger. Few things are more agonizing

than the day you decide to leave them behind in order to save yourself.

But you never stop hoping, one day, they will get to safety, too.

MOTHER

I could write my entire story with my mother as a shadow character, an appendage to my father's will and nothing more. But that wouldn't be anywhere close to accurate, as for most of my life, my mother was my hero.

I grew up with tales of her high school and college experiences, enough to make me jealous she got to be a cheerleader and go to homecoming. Folks who'd gone to school with her confirmed she'd been popular in high school. Her college roommates were still some of her best friends, and she spent a weekend with them every year, back at their alma mater, where the tales of their experiences never seemed to end. Even when I heard the same stories a dozen times, I never grew tired of them.

She ran track in college, and I still have her track jacket, though I haven't worn it in years. Whenever I did, at least one person would say it was cool. They'd ask me if I ran track. I'd say no, but my mother did. That was the next best thing.

She was the sort of mom we enjoyed having around our friends. While she was typically laying out the snacks and didn't stick around for long, she'd always engage and join in the fun. She could talk to our friends in a way that wasn't weird. I think a lot of it came from the fact that she didn't need validation from teenagers. Like she was secure all on her own. And I think this attracted people to her.

She wasn't above a good fart joke or saying the word *boobs*. She took me to buy my first bra, and when I turned thirteen, she took me to get a makeover and bought me my first set of foundation, blush, and mascara. I wasn't even thinking about makeup at thirteen, but my mother bought it for me, so I wore it, because that is what women do.

I enjoyed being her partner in taking care of my younger siblings. I enjoyed her praise for my ability to nurture.

She used to tell us about how she didn't want to get married because she didn't know anyone whose marriage she wanted to emulate. Funny, that sounded a lot like something I said in my twenties and thirties. I wondered what happened to that independent woman who'd light up a room and breeze easily in and out of conversations with men and women alike.

She also used to say she wanted to marry a strong man or else she'd run all over him. I used to think this about myself until I remembered this was what my mother used to say. Her desire for strength was part of the reason she married a controlling man. A strong woman was someone who needed to be reined in and brought to heel. A woman leading the home was against the created order, so my mom was righteous for looking for a man to lead her.

She said she became a Christian in college. Her mom, Nana, was Catholic. To my parents, Catholic did not count as Christian. Though once when I interviewed Nana for a grad school paper about Catholicism, Nana informed me she used to pray to Mary the Mother of Jesus, asking for protection for her daughters and that Mary was who led my mother and my aunt to Christ.

Parents will have their own narratives, despite what their children say.

A child's development is reliant on caregivers. A secure attachment to at least one parent is often enough to help a child grow up securely attached. I remember genuine connection and attachment to my mother. I remember affection. Though I rarely speak to her these days, I have a hole of longing in my body, hoping, waiting, wanting her to one day wake up.

MILES BY MIDNIGHT

Our family loved adventures, the long drives through the night to reach an exotic place. When a few children became driving age, there were plenty of drivers to trade off, sometimes swapping at a gas station in the middle of the night while the rest of the family slept on in the bench seats of the fifteen-passenger van.

My favorite driving partner was Macey. We never ran out of things to talk about. She also had great taste in music and was as equally willing as I was to hide our secular songs from the ears of our father. We'd keep the music low and stifle our laughter so we wouldn't wake our parents.

One night, we missed an exit. It was two in the morning, and we knew our father would give us hell if he were to find out how many miles off course we went. Macey retrieved the atlas and plotted out a way to get back to the right path. We cut through some back roads, and I may have broken one of my father's biggest driving rules (and committed one of the worst sins) by going seven miles per hour over the speed limit (five was all he deemed acceptable).

We made it back to our route and arrived at our destination in a decent amount of time. Nobody knew, and we were giddy from our secret.

I can't remember which trip that was. We went on so many as a family, even internationally: hiking Angels

Landing in Zion, visiting a replica of the Mayflower in New England, eating gelato in Italy and falafel in Israel.

I considered myself lucky to be part of such a family. I loved seeing new places and experiencing different cultures. I loved trying new foods, and I loved creating memories with my siblings.

There was a short time in my adulthood where my parents were pleased with me. My behavior induced so much pride from them. When I was twenty-two, they trusted me enough to leave me with my five younger siblings while they went to Turkey before meeting us in Israel. I brought all my younger siblings overseas, navigating customs with multiple minors in tow.

There was a short time where I really liked my life.

I believed I was happy.

A precious few people saw behind the curtain. At that same age of twenty-two, Naomi, the friend who'd rescued me the night my father kicked me out of the house, pointed to our family Christmas card on her refrigerator. It was taken on a lovely fall day on my parents' property. We stood in the woods, surrounded by a carpet of brown and gold leaves. Our black lab, Cindy, sat casually in front, staring into the camera like she was one of the humans. Our smiles were large, and you'd think fun was the forefront characteristic of our family.

"That photo is such a lie," Naomi said. "All the people in that photo are miserable."

This instigated a torrent of confusing emotions. Because I remember the day we posed for the photo. We were laughing. Cracking jokes.

We were happy, then.

I have learned that when trying to capture the complexity of one's own family, holding the good with the bad is far more challenging when the bad is really bad. To acknowledge the good seems to minimize the bad. But to leave out the good seems to deny the one part of the story that allowed you to survive.

On one of the road trips through the night, we stopped at a gas station. My father was driving and ran inside to use the restroom. Normally everyone would be asleep for this sort of quick stop, but for some reason, everyone woke up.

Our father disliked what he called "unwholesome speech." Curse words were most certainly not allowed. Other outlawed words included *fart* (though *toot* was an acceptable substitute). Language for most private body parts was forbidden.

He also prohibited the bodily act of farting and burping, except on special occasions. We were a family of mostly women, so our fascination with burps and farts contradicted stereotypes, especially because my mother was known to join in when we engaged in such nonsense.

On this night during the road trip, as soon as the door closed behind my father, Macey said, "Quick, Dad's inside. Everybody say something dirty!"

As if the words were waiting on the tip of his tongue, ten-year-old Richard shouted, "Boobies and vaginas!"

We erupted in laughter, and Macey playfully chided Richard. "I meant something like fart or burp."

"Oh my," my mother interjected. "I was thinking dirt or mud."

"Yeah, right!" we chorused in response. My mother was worse than any of us at unwholesome speech.

Our subsequent laughter was compounded by the hysteria of exhaustion. We outwardly sobered when my father returned to the car, though sputters of giggles continued to puff through our lips as we all tried to go back to sleep.

These were the sorts of memories that bring warmth along with them. I remember them more vividly than the memories on the edge of the Grand Canyon or riding a camel outside of Jerusalem.

These were the indelible memories, the ones in a parking lot of a gas station, where we enjoyed shared humor.

That, and the euphoria of collectively defying our father.

MOTIVES

It was another email forwarded from my mother. From Revive Our Hearts ministry. I was sitting at my desk in the open-concept office of my workplace, located in the area of Washington, D.C., known as Chinatown. My first church job after grad school.

I sighed, deleting the email with the subject line "The Faithfulness of God." The last email was about "A Bitter Heart." Normally I just opened them so they weren't bold in my inbox, but left them unread. Lately I'd taken to deleting them as soon as they showed up.

It took me many years to decide why I didn't like Nancy Leigh DeMoss Wolgemuth at Revive Our Hearts. I chalked it up to a dislike of her personality. She'd taken the place of someone I once respected, Elisabeth Elliot (author of influential evangelical books such as *Passion and Purity*) at Revive Our Hearts. So for a while, Elisabeth's name protected Nancy's reputation.

While it may be true that Nancy had Elisabeth's endorsement, I no longer respect Elisabeth Elliot's teachings the way I once did after learning how damaging her teaching on marriage has been to many of my peers, so Nancy sank lower and lower in my estimation. Every time I got an email from my mother forwarded from Revive Our Hearts, I cringed.

In my early thirties, while I was living in D.C., she sent me one celebrating how Nancy had finally gotten married. She told me, "I could just cry!" The subliminal message was *Don't give up hope, Katherine. God can bring a man at any time.*

All I could focus on was how if my future husband looked like a caricature of a serial killer, I'd say, "No, thanks. Return to sender."

Seriously, I thought Nancy's husband looked creepy.

Of course, I felt guilty for assuming my mother's motives. Maybe she truly was just happy and wanted to share the good news with me. Maybe she wasn't trying to send me any subtle messages. But I couldn't forget the email she'd forwarded to me about bitterness when I'd been kicked out of the house and did not return for eight weeks. I felt a lot of things during those weeks (fear, confusion, doubt), but bitterness was not one of them.

My mother made a habit of giving people books or sending them articles about things she thought they needed to hear. I've heard friends and family members express how awkward they felt when they received a forwarded email or a book from her. Maybe she was innocent in all of it, but if a parenting book arrived just after she'd discussed parenting with one of my cousins, it wasn't hard to trace the origin of this "gift."

When I began to realize how much her books and articles caused a sting and left me feeling icky, I resisted doing the same to friends. Even if I found a book I really thought they would like, I kept it to myself. Receiving religious paraphernalia from my mother had always felt like the sermon she would never preach herself, deferring to the experts. Only her choice of experts tended to have a flavor of bullying people with the Bible.

I was in my mid-thirties when I realized books and articles are not—in themselves—the problem. The difficulty lay in the motive. My mother didn't give me information she thought I would like. She gave me material *she* thought I needed.

Even after I asked her to stop sending me Revive Our Hearts material, she continued to send it. "I don't like Revive Our Hearts," I finally said, inwardly cringing because I didn't want to hurt her feelings.

Still the emails came.

"I think they are legalistic," I finally explained—again, worried I'd hurt her feelings.

Still the emails came.

"Please don't send me these anymore. I only delete them."

The emails finally stopped.

Why did I have to ask three times, and why *did I have to be so explicit to get any action?*

Then my mother came to visit me in D.C. At that time, I'd been in therapy for about two years and it had been about five years since I'd left my parents' home. I was just starting to realize what I had experienced growing up was abuse, though I wasn't using that word freely yet. It felt too dramatic. I was aware I did not enjoy talking to my father, and I dodged his phone calls, but I still held affection for my mother.

Our time together was fine, but I do remember she wanted to pray with me one night before going to bed. I felt all kinds of uncomfortable, as I did not want to pray with her, but I could not fathom why. I worked for a church, after all; praying was a pretty significant part of my life. Why did praying with my mother make me so uncomfortable?

I let her do the talking, but doing so somehow felt like I'd given her fodder to excuse any future problems we might have with my lack of spiritual ardor. I wasn't traumatized from childhood, she'd say—I just didn't love God the way I should.

As she was leaving that weekend, out came a shiny hardcover book with a shimmering white dust jacket. "I know you don't like Revive Our Hearts," she said. "But I thought this book was really good."

I glanced at the title: *Adorned*. Nancy's most recent work. I wish I'd had the guts to say, "Mom, please take that book home with you. I won't read it." But I still wanted to believe she was innocent and had good intentions.

The book stayed in the back seat of my car until the next time I went to Goodwill.

A few years later, after a scales-falling-off incident involving my younger brother, Richard, I suddenly became aware of who my mother really was. My whole life, I'd wanted to believe she was just a victim of my father, but something happened that caused me to realize she had become (or maybe always has been) an abuser, too.

THE LETTER

I consider myself lucky I was on the West Coast during the worst of the pandemic. The year-round sunny skies meant no matter how closed down the city was, I could still go outside. I can't imagine a city in lockdown while living in a place with a harsh winter.

Eight years after I'd left my parents' home, in the silence of summer 2020, I wrote my mother a letter.

Dear Mom,

There are some things to be said. My heart is wrestling with it, because I don't want to dispel an image I had of you. But

I know if I keep that image in my head, it does you and me a disservice. Because the image is not true.

I had an image in my head of you that you were one of [my father's] victims, too. You had no choice in what happened to us, because if you tried to stop it, he would hurt you by hurting us.

The abusers are often abused. My mother was my father's chief henchman. But was she always? How long did she fight for us before giving up? Did he break her down, wear her out, so that her will became so enmeshed with his that her true self no longer existed? Or was it buried so deeply no one could reach it?

You did defend us sometimes. I can't ignore that. I can't ignore the truly beautiful moments when you were just my mom. When we laughed or cried together or you gave me good advice. You have genuine empathy, and I did experience it growing up.

Your empathy is what makes you different from [my father], which is why I am writing a letter to you when I haven't written one to [him]. I do not believe a letter to him would do any good. But I believe there's a chance it'll do some good for you.

My mother truly had the capacity for compassion. I believe I felt genuine love from her. Yet somewhere around the time all the grown children had moved away, she grew less and less reasonable. Less and less human. We all noticed it. It showed up in the dwindling, exhausted features of her body and in her behavior. She seemed unable to see boundaries or treat her adult children with any sort of respect.

I think I believed once all the children were gone that she would leave him. I really thought she would leave him. I believed, deeply in my bones, that she only stayed to provide a layer of sanity and protection between the children and her husband.

But she didn't leave. She stayed. She stayed to serve him and even said jokingly, when family acquaintances suggested she get a job now that her children were gone, "Taking care of my husband is a full-time job."

He was, indeed, a full-time job. We children witnessed how she waited on him hand and foot. I knew acutely that the only person in the family who had it worse than I did was my mother. I could escape him at night, in the protection of my own room. She could never get away from him.

I thought you were like me—powerless, without any choices—[but] I now realize you were not like me. Where I was a child who wasn't allowed to grow up, you were always an adult. You married that man with eyes wide open. You saw his abuse with eyes wide open. You assisted his abuse with eyes wide open.

And you were the author of your own abuse—independent of [my father].

And that is why I am writing this letter.

Over ten years ago now, [he] kicked me out of your house because I wouldn't quit a job I'd taken without his permission.

You sent me letters and even said in person that I was rebellious. You said I was spitting in your face. You said you couldn't trust me. You used scripture to condemn and shame me. You sent me articles about having a bitter heart.

I pictured [my father] standing over your shoulder, telling you to say those things. I've had this image in my head for so long, I didn't even question it, because there wasn't any space for me to believe I had two parents who would harm me the way that you did.

But then, just a few years ago, [Richard] told you a terrible secret. He told you how he'd been sexually assaulted by a family friend. He confronted [our father] for his hand in the creation of the situation that made the abuse possible. He was having a difficult time being around [our father], processing the role [our father] played. I know this feeling all too well. [Richard] just needed space.

I called you and asked you not to come to Nana's house for dinner—to give [Richard] the space he needed. On the phone with me, you accused [Richard] of exaggerating. I remember you said, "[Richard] always does this. He blows up. And then he calms down."

By these words, you invalidated your abused child.

Then you disregarded the boundary I created. You [both] came to Nana's anyway. I know [my father]. He's very intelligent, but he's not a good actor. I knew by his behavior you didn't even tell him I asked you not to come. And though you tried to act normal and apologetic for your behavior, you clearly protected [my father] from the pain he should have rightly felt.

And I realized, in that moment, the woman who I thought was a victim, who I desperately wanted to believe was brainwashed by my father, the woman I thought, if given the opportunity,

*would do the right thing, was not the woman I thought
she was.*

*You spent your whole marriage making excuses for [my father].
I spent my whole life making excuses for you.*

*This letter is about our relationship. It is to declare that I see
you now for who you are. You are a woman with good intentions, but I believe your good intentions disappear when it
comes to protecting your husband and the image of your family.*

*I am your daughter, but you chose loyalty to your abusive
husband over your responsibility to protect your child.*

The letter closed with my declaration that I could no longer trust
her. I gave her boundaries. I did not ask for a response.

*I know from your previous behavior that you do not respect
my beliefs [or] my ability to walk in accordance with my
beliefs. That's fine. You don't have to respect me. But these are
my boundaries, and if you cross them I will respond first by
reminding you of this letter.*

I read the letter to my mother over the phone. I asked her not to
speak or interrupt me. I told her I was getting off the phone as soon
as I finished reading and that I would email her the letter so she
could have a copy.

Two months later, she responded with a separate email.

She DARVOed me.

DARVO stands for Deny, Attack, and Reverse Victim and
Offender.

I am so grieved that you have held this anger and pain
in for so long.

It's common practice for the person who abused us to blame us for
how long we waited to talk to them, rather than acknowledging the
actual words we say.

My mother completely disregarded the things I said in my letter.
She created a scenario where we were both at fault.

She ended her letter with an offer to meet to discuss ways she
had offended me, though I'd already outlined several items in the
previous letter that she did not even mention. It was as if those
things did not count.

Let's both pray and come to this with willingness to forgive and
move forward in love.

It is common for the person who abused us to try to create a scenario where we are both equally responsible, when really, they consider us most responsible. Slowly but surely, they make us out to
be the guilty party.

In previous email exchanges with my mother, I was always
apologetic and dutifully submissive. I told my mother how much I
loved her, trying to assuage any pain I might cause her. But in my
final response, I was firm that there was no reason to meet. I was
not writing to try to work things out. I reminded her that I'd given
her a list of things to consider. I told her I expected her to honor
my boundaries.

I don't see any reason for us to meet face-to-face for me to try
to go into more details and try to make you understand. I gave
examples. And if you cannot see from those examples how you
have contributed to the hurt and shame in our family, there is
nothing else I can do.

I am glad I wrote this last letter. I believe I wrote it mostly for my-self so I know with certainty that she knows what she did.

In some states, if one person in a marriage is abusive, the children will be taken away from both parents. The parent who stays in the abusive marriage is considered unsafe while they remain with their abusive partner. Exposing your child to abuse is considered abuse.

My mother was an adult with a responsibility to protect her children. I believe I cannot excuse her negligence or abuse on the grounds that she was also abused.

While I remain firm in this, I still have a lingering longing that my mother will one day find freedom. The difference is that now I do not feel responsible for helping her on that road. I'm the daughter. It's not my job to save my mother.

But that doesn't mean I don't still shed tears and desperately wish that somehow I could.

MORTAL ILLNESS

In 2021, I moved back to the Midwest from the West Coast, to the same city where I'd attended graduate school. For a short time, I lived with my friend Martha, who had recently separated from her husband and was beginning the divorce process.

It happened during a trip to the beach, she told me. They were together with their son for a week without the distractions of work and everyday life. They fought the whole time. The illusion shattered, and the relationship began to unravel quickly, though it sounded like it had been unraveling from the beginning—she just hadn't realized it.

Within a few months, she'd moved into an apartment and had filled out the divorce papers. As I heard more stories, it seemed

Martha wasn't just in a marriage that wasn't working. It appeared she was in an abusive marriage.

As I witnessed Martha go through the challenges associated with separating her life from someone she'd been married to for twelve years, I got an inside look at how difficult it is to get divorced, especially if you don't have a separate source of income, which luckily Martha had.

Martha's son was five years old at the time. Yes, it was traumatizing for him to experience the divorce of his parents, but I couldn't help thinking how much more traumatizing it would have been to grow up in a home witnessing abuse.

I know. I'd experienced it. I told Martha this. I have often wondered if I'd have a more hopeful, favorable view of marriage if my mother had divorced my father rather than forcing me to watch her struggle under his mistreatment.

One morning while I was living with Martha, I woke up and experienced a rage come over me. I started sobbing. After Martha left for work, I did a kickboxing workout to get out my aggression.

The source of my rage was watching how Martha, the moment she realized her marriage was over, made a healthy choice for herself and her son and got out. She didn't stick around to try to save it. She shed the Christian admonitions to keep forgiving, over and over, until her entire life was consumed by a man who didn't deserve it. The source of my rage was knowing my mother hadn't done the same thing for me.

The source of the rage went back even further. To my father's mother. My grandmother had also been married to a man I consider abusive. But because of her Christian faith, she stayed put. She literally sacrificed herself for her marriage. I believe her marriage killed her.

My grandmother died of cancer. She battled it for somewhere around twelve years. First ovarian, then breast, and finally, liver cancer. The last bit ended it.

My grandmother's research into natural healing led to over-hauling her lifestyle. I agree with her and the doctors that her commitment to nutrition probably prolonged her life.

But to what purpose?

During the three months I lived with Martha, I was in school studying trauma. I learned about the correlation between trauma and so many diseases, even potentially terminal ones like cancer. The amount of stress on a body, especially prolonged stress over time, eventually shows up in physical ailments.

It's why we sometimes get sick after we finish finals or after we go through a big life transition. Our body is storing up the stress, and then it just shuts down.

In their book *Burnout: The Secret to Unlocking the Stress Cycle*, Emily and Amelia Nagoski write,

> *Let's think about what [stress] does to just one system, the cardio-vascular: Chronically activated stress response means chronically increased blood pressure, which is like constantly turning a firehose on in your blood vessels, when those vessels were designed by evolution to handle only a gently flowing stream. The increased wear and tear on your blood vessels leads to increased risk for heart disease. That's how chronic stress leads to life-threatening illness.*

If we never get a chance to recover from stress, it builds up. Then it kills us.

After my grandmother's death, I remember my mother saying about my grandfather, "He killed her." She was weeping when she said it. Now, she probably would be mortified that she said it (and definitely that I remember it), but it was probably the most honest thing she ever said about our family.

My grandfather was known for being a difficult man. My grand-mother was cast in the role of saint. Everyone loved her. She was a beacon of patience and virtue in her church community. If she'd divorced him, she would have been a pariah—as is so often the case for women who leave their husbands, especially a few decades ago. She likely would have been destitute because she had no college degree and had been a homemaker while she raised her kids.

When my father touted the new vision for our family, that his daughters wouldn't go to college and would stay home to prepare to be wives and mothers, I remember my grandmother saying to me, "I really wish he'd let you go to college."

I know she regretted not having a degree. I wonder if she regretted it because it would have been a way out. I doubt it. She was committed to that marriage. She was committed to suffering. In the end, she was committed to martyrdom.

In that moment of rage, punching it out in Martha's living room, I did not admire my grandmother for her suffering. I did not admire my mother. I was angry at both my mother and grandmother for trying to be so holy they subjected their children to abuse.

I'll be charitable here and say I don't think my grandmother knew it was abuse. I know she didn't, because she never named it that. She saw what sort of man my father was and never called it abuse. When she told me she wished my father would let me go to college, she said she'd thought about talking to him about it. "But he won't listen to me. Because I'm a woman."

After I'd finished my workout in Martha's living room, I took a shower and several deep breaths. Rational thought seeped back in. Both my grandmother and mother were homemakers with children. They didn't have careers outside of their family, the way Martha did. They lived in communities and in a different generation that didn't support divorce. They didn't have the research that supported the health of raising a child as a single parent over raising them partnered when the partner was abusive.

They both were extremely religious and believed God wanted them to save their husbands "without a word," citing 1 Peter 3:1 to validate their submission. I believe they both did the best they could with the knowledge and resources they had. I don't believe either wanted their children to be collateral damage.

Yet I must hold this belief alongside my desires. I wish they would have left their husbands. I wish they would have said to themselves, "I deserve better." I wish they would have chosen health for themselves and their children.

I wish they would have dared to believe they could have a better ending.

SEVEN: EMOTIONS

Conceal, Don't Feel

BYPASSING

Somewhere around tenth grade, I attended a funeral for the father of a homeschool friend. Whatever branch of Christianity this family came from sought to treat funerals as a celebration. Their loved one was now safe in heaven with Jesus. This wasn't a loss; it was a party! They kept sharing the message that Jesus provided hope in death—attempting to lead the crowd of onlookers into a relationship with that Christ.

The daughter of the deceased man was my friend. She played a song during the service; I can't remember which one, but it was a jolly tune. Everyone was smiling, laughing, and celebrating. I found it strange. Then I felt bad for thinking this response was strange, as they were pointing people to Jesus (or so it seemed).

Spiritual bypassing is a term that describes when someone minimizes or overlooks genuine pain with a spiritual outlook. For example: Someone confesses to struggling after they have been laid off from a job. Their well-meaning aunt might say something like, "God works in mysterious ways. You never know what danger being laid off saved you from." This ignores the very real difficulty of losing a job, even one you might eventually be glad is over.

I know a number of friends, acquaintances, and clients who lost their faith after losing a child, or after watching a friend or loved one lose a child. Or this loss catapulted them on a long journey of questioning and struggling with Christianity. The common spiritual bypassing statements they've heard from Christians consist of things like "Don't you know that Jesus suffered, too?" (Is a man suffering two thousand years ago supposed to ease present-day suffering?)

"There is a reason for everything." (Is this supposed to comfort someone aching from horrible loss?)

"God wanted another angel." (As Nicole Kidman's character in the film *Rabbit Hole* says, "Why didn't he just make one?")

While spiritual bypassing can be incredibly painful for the one receiving it, it helps me to remember that the person who is doing the spiritual bypassing isn't actually thinking about me when they do it. Rather, they do not have the internal resources to sit with uncomfortable emotions or the uncertainty of inexplicable suffering. So they say things like this to momentarily ease their own anxiety—it isn't about me at all.

This is the same for someone who might spiritually bypass themselves. The parent who says "God wanted another angel" to console themselves after the loss of a child is likely in the denial stage of their grief. They aren't ready to deal with the onslaught of emotions that accompany this seemingly senseless loss. And you know what? That's perfectly okay. They can spiritually bypass themselves as long as they need to in order to get through the day.

But spiritual bypassing is problematic when it's a cultural norm. This is a significant problem in evangelicalism. Spiritual bypassing is embedded into the system, but people often call it faith. Cheerful yet superficial responses to death, loss, and sorrow are considered trusting the Lord.

One day, my homeschool friend who played the song at her father's funeral was going to encounter the reality that her beloved father was dead. She'd want to, and need to, experience the grief, but her brand of Christianity wouldn't allow it. Instead, she'd stuff it way down, spiritually bypassing herself like a good little Christian.

And all that trauma would get stored in her body, showing up in other ways—as trauma is wont to do—be it physical ailments, emotional outbursts, struggles in relationships, or any number of symptoms. She would never address them, however. She'd just keep surrendering all the suffering and struggles to God, never actually sifting through the genuine human emotions she was designed and meant to feel.

One of the primary things I struggled with in my first years of therapy was allowing myself to feel those challenging emotions. Anger. Sadness. Confusion. The culture of spiritual bypassing I'd grown up in not only prevented me from feeling them, it also communicated, quite loudly, that those emotions are bad.

It's difficult to feel something you have been conditioned to believe is wrong.

PHOBIAS

The eight weeks I lived with Nana and negotiated with my parents after being kicked out of their home were excruciating with uncertainty and fear. Yet those eight weeks helped me with something I hadn't known I needed. One of my greatest fears had always been getting cut off from my family. My greatest fear had come upon me, and I had survived. Actually, it wasn't as terrible as I thought it might be. I enjoyed the freedom of those eight weeks. I got to experience a life without surveillance. I discovered I quite liked it.

Then I returned home to my parents' house, determined to accumulate the necessary resources so the next time I left, I would never go back.

I did not write my escape plan on paper. But that didn't mean I hadn't hatched one that was calculated with meticulous precision. The bare bones of it went like this:

1. Get another job (the part-time one at the church wasn't enough to pay for college).
2. Buy a car (and pay it off as soon as possible).
3. Get a college degree (as quickly and as quietly as possible as an online student).
4. Move out.

While I was enacting this plan, I had a few rules:

1. Do not talk to Dad about college, the future, money, or anything that might tip him off.
2. Smile and act like everything is fine whenever you are around Dad.
3. Stay away from the house (and away from Dad) as much as possible.
4. Don't tell anyone about your plan. Ever.

That eight weeks with Nana gave me an unexpected gift. For once in my relationship with my father, I had the upper hand. For the rest of my time living with my parents, my father handled me carefully. Whenever he was around, he was syrupy nice and would say my nickname in a singsongy voice whenever he saw me. "Blue Eyes!" he'd chime. I'd indulge him with a smile (and occasionally a hug), while inside I felt dead.

On Valentine's Day, he left roses in my room. I remember wishing he hadn't. At the same time, I felt bad that I didn't want the flowers. I calculated how many days I had to leave them in that vase atop my desk before I could safely throw them away without him noticing. But I told him "Thank you for the flowers," with minimal enthusiasm in my voice. If I ignored the flowers and tossed them like I wanted to, it would tip him off that his ingratiation wasn't working, and he might turn mad again.

I needed to keep my father docile and pliable. I needed to keep him happy while he thought he was keeping me happy. It was a part of the plan.

A few months after I'd completed college, just two years after getting kicked out of the house, my friend Anne (who had just turned twenty-six and was still living with her parents) asked me to move in with her for a couple months while her parents were traveling.

It was the perfect opportunity to leave home temporarily.

Nobody had to know that I had no intention of going back.

It was nighttime when I packed most of my essential belongings and loaded the car I'd finally paid off. It was important for my plan that I owned 100 percent of that car when I left. I couldn't leave behind anything my father could use against me.

However, a few months after leaving, my father gave me a piece of paper with numbers typed in a list—itemized arbitrary expenses. I knew what it was, as a couple of my siblings had received similar lists when they tried to move out. It was a list of items I owed him money for. Because my father had a pattern of slapping his children with a hefty bill at the time when they were attempting to assert their independence, this was likely a calculated form of financial abuse—deliberately using money to coerce and control. I learned about this form of abuse much later on in life.

I don't know what was on the list he gave me because I threw it away the minute I realized what it was. I knew he couldn't force that money from me. We didn't have a contract, and I wasn't relying on him financially anymore. He didn't have anything he could use against me. He'd already used up all his leverage.

Nobody was home the night I left, so I didn't have to explain why I was carrying suitcases down the stairs and out to my car, but that didn't keep me from hastening my departure, sweating in the January cold as I moved swiftly to be able to get in that car and drive away.

I had a cover story in case one of my family members arrived home unexpectedly and saw me. I'd tell them the truth: Anne's parents were out of town for two months, and she'd asked me to keep her company. The truth was, I was willing to live in my car before ever returning to my parents. I didn't tell anyone this part of my escape plan, not even my sisters or Anne. They needed to have deniability if questioned.

About a decade later, I learned about phobias—extreme bouts of fear that sometimes can follow leaving a high-control religious environment. People usually describe it as fear of God striking them down by lightning. It can present as panic, heart palpitations, sleeplessness, and convulsions. Typically, your mind begins drawing up horrible possible catastrophes that might befall you—the worst of which is that God has rejected you and you will never again return to his good graces.

That first night at Anne's, I lay awake for hours, weeping and hyperventilating. Tears rolled down my face, and I tossed and turned in bed. Then I got up and began pacing as intrusive thoughts bubbled through my brain like lava out of a volcano.

Nobody saw me leave. Nobody knows I'm gone. I could pack up my stuff right now and go back home. Nobody has to know I left. If I don't go now, I could always go tomorrow and just say I was spending the night at Anne's. Oh, but what would Anne say? I told her I'd stay with her for two months. She'll be so disappointed. But she'll understand. She'll understand pleasing your parents. But she doesn't know I didn't tell them I was leaving. She doesn't know I'm not planning to go back. She won't understand. Oh God, what did I just do?

The phobia was strong. So very strong. I almost went back.

Then I remembered the pastor who'd told me the average abused woman leaves seven times before she leaves for good.

Then I remembered my plan and how much time I'd put into it.

Then I remembered how hard I'd worked to get to this place. I'd come too far to undo it all by going back.

I crawled back in bed, cocooned myself beneath the blankets, and cried myself to sleep.

SUPPRESSION

"I know there's no way that what I experienced growing up didn't impact me," I said during my first session with a new therapist. "But the only thing that feels off is dating. I've never dated anyone. That's the only evidence I can find right now."

I was twenty-nine. It had been three years since the night I moved out of my parents' home. I wasn't yet using the word *abuse* to describe my experience with my family of origin. But it wasn't because of denial. I *wanted* someone to tell me it was abuse. I wanted someone to tell me it was as bad as I felt like it was. But because I'd never been raped, never been starved (aside from the usual punishment of having to skip dinner), never been punched in the face by my father, I didn't quite know what to call what I'd experienced. I just knew it wasn't good.

I arrived in seminary straight from the mission field after a year in Mexico. Seminary had an in-house counseling program and free therapy for students if you saw one of the interns. I'd wanted to go to therapy for years. I just couldn't afford it. Free therapy was the best gift seminary gave me.

My desires for marriage—or really the deep desire that some man would want me badly enough to duck past the glaring "Fuck off" flashing across my forehead—was the key reason I wanted to go to therapy. From an outside perspective, I looked like a normal, healthy human. I kept jobs. I had friends. I got good grades. I'd made it into grad school, and I was one of few students who had a job in ministry while also attending seminary (a coveted combination). Dating was the only thing in my life I could name as not going well.

At nearly thirty years old, I felt I should have had at least one boyfriend. Or at least one experience where the stars aligned in such a way that I liked someone who actually liked me back.

Boys had liked me and asked me out, but no one I was ever remotely interested in. I'd thought about dating them just because, but the thought of marrying them made me sick to my stomach. Guys I liked never liked me back. Not only did they not like me back, they didn't give me the time of day. Part of the reason for this might be that as soon as I liked a guy—or saw him as even the smallest potential of a prospect—I melted into this cowardly dunce who couldn't string sentences together. Sometimes I felt like my body was sabotaging me on purpose. I'd leave encounters with minor crushes and ask myself, *What was* that? This pattern increased the mortification and shame I already felt around men I found attractive.

All that to say, this was the one minor wrinkle I brought with me to therapy, a tidy problem offered on a platter to my therapist so she'd think I deserved to be there. I did not want her to feel like she was wasting her time when other people had *real* problems. I acknowledged it was likely I hadn't escaped my upbringing unscathed. I just didn't know exactly how it impacted me, so dating was the problem I focused on.

Deep down, I knew I was messed up. I held myself together with the tightest of bindings in the form of perfectionism, though few people would have called me a perfectionist. I was clumsy and awkward and most definitely quirky. I committed social faux pas without awareness. I said dumb things and only emerged as cool when I was surrounded by other uncool people who made me look good. Yet I prided myself on my hypercontrol of my emotions. On regular days, I could shut off unpleasant emotions like flipping a switch, giving my own mother the opportunity to call me stoic and selfish.

But I knew this control had an expiration date. I felt I was wound so tight that something might send me into a fit of rage that could end in serious injury. I'd scared myself once as an adolescent when we were building my father's house on a Saturday. In the structure that would become my parents' bedroom suite, my father was standing on a ladder near the edge of the whirlpool tub he was about to install, showing me how to connect the wires of can lights in the ceiling. I had a sudden vision of my father falling from the ladder and breaking his neck. The vision terrified me so much that I walked to the other side of the tub.

It was not the first or last time I imagined how much easier my life would be if my father would just die.

I felt the rage inside me, but during my first session of therapy, it didn't have a name. I'd grown up with an aversion to expressions of anger. I wrongly thought anger was only explosive and sometimes violent—which was how I experienced my father's anger.

I now know that anger comes in many forms. The absence of an outward expression does not mean someone isn't housing rage in their body.

In those first few sessions of therapy, I felt that if I got too close to the sleeping beast inside of me, it would awaken, snarling and rabid. I thought I might kill someone. Or burst into an onset of body-quaking sobs, a tide that once begun would not stop until it destroyed everything in its path—including me.

I did not know then how very close to the truth I was.

WHY I CHEERED FOR DEATH

"Is it wrong that I'm this excited about murder?" I wiped tears of joy from my eyes and punched the air, yelling,

"Yes, queen!" at the TV screen. Lagertha, my favorite character from the History Channel show *Vikings,* had just stabbed her fiancé in the heart.

But let me tell you the backstory and why I cheered and shed tears of happiness upon witnessing this brutal death.

Lagertha was married to the show's main character, Ragnar, who eventually becomes an earl and, later, king. Ragnar impregnates another woman, and he wants to cohabitate with both his wife and the other woman.

Lagertha essentially says, "Nope, not gonna happen." She leaves Ragnar (a moment I felt extremely proud of her). Because women can't really survive without male protection and because Lagertha has her own son to think of, she marries another earl. This earl beats her and rapes her, and Lagertha repays his kindness with a knife in his eye, thereby claiming his earldom and becoming the only female earl of the series to that point.

Lagertha rules as earl and turns down many offers of marriage. She entrusts her earldom to her right-hand man when she goes raiding (like Vikings do). When she gets back, her right-hand man has usurped her earldom. Her ex, Ragnar (who is now king), refuses to help her get it back.

While raiding again, the right-hand-turned-betrayer tells Lagertha that he desires her. She responds by telling him she's happy for them to become lovers, as long as he's fully aware that one day she will kill him. He doesn't seem to have a problem with this, and the two become an item.

A few years go by and Lagertha's new lover mag-
nanimously seeks to share the earldom with Lagertha.
He even kills anyone who is against her ruling as his
equal. Eventually he proposes to Lagertha and she
accepts, at which point my heart kind of sank.
I said to my watching buddy, "Doesn't she remember
that he stole the earldom from her?"

Apparently, Lagertha heard me, because she
decides to kill her right-hand-turned-betrayer-turned-
lover-turned-fiancé on their wedding day. She
completes her long game by walking among her
people, wedding dress covered in blood, surrounded
by women who she trained as warriors as they
proclaim her earl.

This is why I cheered. In a world of violence and
betrayal where women were often at the mercy of more
powerful men, Lagertha took her life back, empowering
other women along the way.

EXPOSURE THERAPY

The intern therapist I'd been seeing at seminary graduated and
wasn't planning to start a practice right away. Even if she had, I
couldn't afford it. I began seeing a new intern, but I eventually
stopped seeing her because her expression of emotions was even
more muted than mine. I also felt like she was overwhelmed by my
story. Considering expressing my emotions was already the crux of
what I was now exploring on my journey, I couldn't be with someone who was more reserved than I was.

I also couldn't be with a therapist who contributed to my feeling
that I was too much. I already refrained from revealing significant

pieces of my life because I knew it was too much for the normal world to handle. I just couldn't bear to feel this way in therapy.

I'm not sure what prompted the idea or what gave me the gumption to pursue it, but I broached the subject with an administrative staff. I asked if it were possible to see a male therapist who had experience with survivors of abuse. After a year in therapy, I was growing more accustomed to using the word *abuse*, though I still felt like I was being too dramatic.

The administrative staff wisely suggested it might be better if I saw someone who was not an intern. My school gave me a scholarship, and the person the counseling program recommended gave me a small discount. I ended up paying $25 a session. For someone living on $900 a month, this was exorbitant. However, after a year in therapy, I felt like I was just beginning to scratch the surface of exploring the impact of my upbringing. The next step was dealing with my issues with men.

With the help of therapy and a regular yoga practice, I became attuned enough with my body to recognize a slight panicking reaction whenever I was in the presence of men, even if my cognitive brain told me these particular men were safe (my definition of safety was quite limited back then). Considering I was highly skilled at suppressing emotions, I never allowed this panic to overwhelm me, but I could no longer ignore it.

Here's a great idea, I thought. *Let's nip this in the bud and see a male therapist.* The experience would fix me, I was sure.

Years later, my sister Irene would ask me what it was like to see a male therapist, as she was thinking of seeing one as a form of exposure therapy. I responded, "It was very disruptive, but I made a lot of progress."

This is still how I would describe it.

ANGER

I sat on the therapist's couch, my left hand gripping a throw pillow in my lap. The pillow covered my right hand, which was involuntarily scrunched into a fist.

During one of our first sessions, my male therapist suggested I begin exploring women's anger. I bit back my usual retort that I wasn't angry, because I was starting to notice a pattern. Several years before, a family friend had asked me why I was angry at my father. I said I wasn't angry; I was frustrated. He replied, "Frustration *is* anger."

Oh.

My previous therapist suggested I was angry, but what I felt did not compute with the expressions of anger I was accustomed to seeing. That anger was all yelling and screaming. Demeaning and sometimes physical violence. I didn't do any of those things. But this male therapist made the connection. "Women's anger often looks different than the anger of men."

Oh.

I emerged from my exploration finally convinced I was angry, and my anger was nothing to be ashamed of.

A few sessions later, I showed my therapist my right hand, the one that had been balled in a fist in my lap. Each session, my fist would scrunch up like that, and one day, when I got home, my unballed fist revealed four bleeding micro-slices in the flesh of my palm, the shapes of half-moons. Indentions left behind by my fingernails.

"It just happens," I said. "I'm not doing it on purpose."

He didn't seem alarmed. "Maybe the next time it happens, ask your hand what it's trying to tell you."

I almost rolled my eyes.

This was my first step into the world of somatic healing, the idea of working with the body to access the stuff our cognitive minds can't reach. The next time my fist involuntarily clenched, I asked it what it was trying to say. While it didn't respond (with words or with any other form of communication), it stopped clenching after that.

I think my body just wanted to know someone was listening.

I would leave sessions with my male therapist even more dis-rupted than I had with the intern therapist, but I also knew things were happ-ening. Stuff was seeping out of the iron chests I'd locked deep inside myself for my survival. That male therapist showed me a few forms of regulating and connecting with my body when I was activated, like box breathing and connecting with the five senses. These are methods I still use to this day. He suggested using these methods whenever I felt the panic arise around men.

One of the most pivotal moments with my therapist was the only time I ever saw *his* anger. A lot of therapists are trained to be emotionless, and I think some are better at it than others. I don't agree with this approach for survivors of trauma. My emotions play a significant role in my work with my clients, though they are never more important than the emotions of my clients. Sometimes trauma survivors need someone to show them how to feel, to show them their feelings are not something to be afraid of.

I had just come to a session straight from a meeting with an elder at the church in the Midwest where I worked. The elder had wanted to talk about a conflict between my coworker and me. The core of the conflict was this: My coworker was a Veritable Ass and terrible at his job. I was very good at the job, and my coworker was limiting what we could do because he was so bad at it.

I did not feel comfortable discussing this with the elder. I know now it was because I didn't feel like he'd earned the right to have access to information about the most troubling situation in my life at the time. But he wanted my intimacy and sat across from me at Panera Bread essentially demanding I disclose my greatest struggle to him. I deflected for the duration of breakfast.

The elder finally gave up, passing over my reticence with the comment, "Well, you're really tight-lipped, aren't you?"

When I got to this part in the story, I saw my therapist grab the arms of his chair. It was an instinctual reaction. His face changed, too. His jaw twitched, and I knew the elder's behavior toward me made him angry.

Forced intimacy is normalized in the church, but that doesn't make it okay.

I don't remember anything else from that session. I only remember this: my therapist's involuntary flinch of rage that a man in a church would contribute to the trauma I was working so hard to heal from. I only remember a man's anger at the way another man had treated me.

I think one of my deepest, unnamed longings throughout my life was to see someone get as pissed at my father—and every other man who'd hurt me—as I was. At the time, I still valued what men thought over and above my own thoughts and feelings. So, to have a man get angry at another man on my behalf? It was probably the most healing moment of our whole year working together.

CONTRADICTION

Most folks spend a lot of time in therapy learning how to feel and navigate their emotions. But folks who come from high-control Christianity have an added layer they must contend with. That layer is the subconscious judgment that any emotion beyond continually praising the Lord isn't worthy of one of his children.

As I mentioned earlier, it's difficult to begin feeling emotions we've been conditioned to see as wrong. The reasons learning about women's anger was so pivotal in my healing journey are twofold. First, I believed anger was dangerous because I'd seen it lead to physical assault. Second, men got a pass when they got angry. Women did not. Women were placated, mocked, or punished for their anger.

In my first childhood home, in the first house I remember, there was a hole in the basement wall paneling. We laughed when we told the story to friends that my older brother Micah, in a fit of rage, had put his fist through the wall. Considering we moved when I was eleven and Micah was thirteen, he was quite young when he punched the wall.

And we laughed about it. Even though I believe my brother was disciplined for the outburst that led to the damage in our basement wall, we laughed about it.

While I was privy to displays of anger from myself, my mother, and my sisters, I never saw any of us break things. I don't believe this is due to female versus male nature. My mother never displayed her anger in physical violence. Sometimes she'd burst into tears and run from the room. I once witnessed her let fly a stream of cuss words that she later apologized for.

My father was a man, and it was culturally acceptable for him to display his rage with physical aggression. My brother was a boy; therefore, he was also allowed to punch a wall when he got angry. At the same time, anger was a contradictory emotion. My father preached sermons to our family on the proper use of anger. "Be angry, and yet do not sin" was a verse from Ephesians my father habitually quoted. He taught that we were allowed to be angry *at* sin. This was the presumed justification for displays of anger against his wife and children: He was angry at our sin.

My sisters and I implicitly knew we had to hide our anger. We had to bottle it up. But that did not mean we didn't have any, as I learned in my near thirties. I was very angry—I just hadn't been allowed to acknowledge it. I certainly wasn't allowed to feel it.

Oh, the sweet compassion I slowly grew to offer myself in my anger. Befriending my rage was one of the most wonderful healing gifts I ever gave to myself. Anger is an active emotion that notifies us we feel something is wrong. Anger calls us to *do something*. When we are angry, we must physically move that anger through our bodies, or else it'll get stuck there and come out in places and by means that are not always helpful—as I witnessed hundreds of times while growing up.

While working at the abusive church on the West Coast, I was awakened in the middle of the night by my next-door neighbors. The thin walls in the apartment complex reverberated with the boom of their party music. It was a Saturday night, and I had to work on Sunday mornings. In a flash of irritation, I jumped out of bed, marched to the kitchen, grabbed a mop, and then marched back to my room. I started banging on my bedroom wall, funneling my rage toward the party that had woken me up.

After about five bangs, I suddenly stopped. With a zap of clarity, I realized I wasn't actually angry at my neighbors. Well, I was a little. This sort of thing would irk anyone. It needed to be addressed, but on a normal night, I might put in earplugs and go sleep on the couch.

I was acutely aware my anger was out of proportion with the need of the moment. The mop and the wall were a conduit for the pent-up rage and powerlessness I was feeling during that season working at the church. I knew it and felt it so clearly. My anger was a sign something was wrong. It needed to be felt and addressed. My anger was just one more bodily sensation telling me that the situation I was in needed to change. I needed to heed my anger, along with all the other signs telling me something at the church wasn't right.

Anger is a wonderful and helpful emotion. Because it is active, when I become angry, I first work out the anger through movement: walking, running, kickboxing. Then, I'm able to navigate the reason for the anger with resources and tools I've learned along the way. I'm more comfortable stating in the moment "That makes me angry" without shame.

I've grown to love and value my anger. And ironically, as I've learned how to exercise my voice by advocating for myself (and others), I've become much less angry.

EIGHT: MARRIAGE

Did They Really Want to Say "I Do"?

JUST CHRISTIANITY

For many years after I left the South, I maintained a relationship with a longtime friend from childhood. She was a mother of young children, homeschooling and rarely alone. We'd occasionally snag a few minutes to talk when she was running errands—the only time she really had by herself.

Once, during a ten-minute phone call, she quoted her husband three times. In ten minutes, she quoted another person thrice. For ten minutes, she didn't even seem to have her own thoughts. I got off the phone and thought, *Christianity creates enmeshed relationships within marriage.*

This wasn't the first time I espoused this theory. Here was an example in real time. My friend wasn't quite as extreme as my parents, who believed homeschooling was the only godly way to raise your children, nor was she someone who thought all women needed to stay home with their kids (at least she didn't think this consciously).

My family imbued me with overt messages about marriage and children, deliberately telling me that to marry, birth children, submit to my husband, and homeschool my children was the godliest of all godly paths. While most of the everyday Christians surrounding us did not say these things openly, the first time I became acquainted with a woman who didn't follow this specific path and instead had a career outside of her family was when I took a job as a nanny for a night nurse. This was when I was twenty-five and attending college without my father's knowledge.

Every other woman I knew while growing up, every woman immediately connected with my family, was a stay-at-home mom. The only exception was the occasional woman who got a part-time job after her children were all grown. But even then, they would make jokes about how it was only to pass the time because they didn't make much money, considering how most of them had gotten married after college and started having children immediately. They never used their college degree. Never had a career. Which only fueled my parents' argument that college was a waste of time for women.

It's important to parse out these subtle and not-so-subtle messages because they are indicative of wider theology and doctrines that intentionally oppress women within certain expressions of Christianity. While I will never say that a woman who stays home with her children while her husband works is throwing her life away (saying this would be a different sort of fundamentalism), I believe it's extremely important to ask the question, if a woman makes this choice, was it *really* her choice?

Even outside of Christianity, it's an accepted reality that if a woman chooses to focus on her career, contingencies are rarely made. She's expected to still be the primary caregiver of children. She often bears the brunt of the housework. She is never paid for emotional labor.

I once checked out the book *Emotional Labor* by Rose Hackman from the library. I got through one chapter and had to put the book down. It was so depressing to realize how the wider world really wasn't much different than the Christian world I'd come from—not in how it treats women. I believe this is evidence of how Christian patriarchy has a strong influence on the world at large. These subtle beliefs are embedded into our bodies and systems.

The main difference between the Christian world and the rest of the world, however, is the wider world does not try to convince you the oppression of women is godly and biblical. It may sideline, silence, and overlook women. It may have horrible laws that support perpetrators of abuse and retraumatize victims. It may continue to put awful men in power. But it doesn't justify this behavior with scripture and a higher power.

The conservative church's teaching on marriage is abusive. It's just been so normalized we think it's Christianity.

SMOOTHIES

The first time I acknowledged I did not want my parents' marriage, I was a preteen. I wasn't much interested in boys, and this was a few years before my first real crush. The closest I got to thinking about weddings and marriage happened when I'd hang out with friends at a local Books-A-Million and we'd flip through bridal magazines, choosing our dresses, cakes, and wedding songs.

But the first time I acknowledged I did not want my parents' marriage I was grabbing a smoothie with my father near that same Books-A-Million. He asked me, rather offhandedly, if I hoped to have a marriage like his and Mom's.

I thought a moment and said, "No, I don't think so."

"What do you mean?" he asked.

I mentioned the only tangible thing I could think of: "I don't like the way you make Mom wait for you to open the door for her." Many times, I'd witnessed my father chiding my mother from the driver's seat when she'd reach for the car door. "Wait," he'd order. Then he'd open his door, come around to her side, and let her out.

To my pragmatic, preteen brain, this seemed illogical and a waste of time.

To my father, however, my comment seemed to step on something sacred. The skin on his face stretched, and his eyes grew big with a mix of anger and hurt. "Did you ever think that maybe your mom *likes* when I open the door for her?"

Oh, I hadn't thought of that. I hadn't thought maybe Mom and Dad had secret conversations. Conversations that sounded something like this:

"Honey," my father would say. "Do you want me to open the car door for you?"

"Sure, that'd be nice."

"Okay, well you'll have to let me."

"Okay."

"Do you want me to remind you when you forget?"

"Sure, baby. Whatever you want."

They'd struck a secret bargain that my child eyes hadn't witnessed. I instantly felt even more childish. How could I possibly understand? Maybe my mom really *did* like it. It was disrespectful of me to think they didn't know what they were doing.

My father and I had our smoothie and returned home. I didn't allow myself to question my parents' marriage again until probably a decade later. This one conversation was loud enough to overtake any thoughts that suspected theirs wasn't a good marriage. Marriage was a sacred thing, wholly beyond my grasp.

Though I believed my father was telling the truth, deep down, I was determined: *If my husband ever asks me if I want him to open the car door for me, I'll tell him no.*

In the years that followed, I often heard both my parents declare how much they loved each other and how fun marriage was. I had no reason to doubt they felt that way about their marriage.

It was very confusing to not like their marriage yet constantly have them tell me it was a good marriage. I wasn't allowed to think badly about their marriage because how they ordered their marriage appeared intricately connected to what they believed God wanted.

To dislike their marriage was to dislike what God intended.

But ever since that day, in the shared parking lot of Books-A-Million and Smoothie King, I knew I didn't want their marriage.

THE ONE WHO DIDN'T GET AWAY

Phillip was a guy in high school who would have received my parents' approval for marriage. He was responsible and respectful and wore button-downs tucked into his khaki pants. He was moderately attractive and had a life plan that involved a stable job and a family. He said things like "I want to be a good leader" when he described what sort of husband he wanted to be. He talked about the Lord. He was homeschooled.

I was terrified I would end up marrying him.

Aside from having a small crush on him for a little while, I really couldn't fathom joining my life to his forever. I was sixteen, and I wondered if my parents would force me to marry Phillip, because this was the first person I'd ever known who would pass their inspection.

Several years later, he started dating someone seriously, news that caused relief and disappointment and a complex assortment of other emotions. Phillip was the sort of person who wouldn't date someone seriously unless he intended to marry them, so barring something out-rageous or tragic, I knew his girlfriend would become his wife.

I felt like I dodged a bullet. I also felt my last hope for marriage was about to amble his way down the aisle with another woman.

While I did not want to marry Phillip, I maintained hope that someday I would want to—or at the very least, that I'd want to marry someone like him. It took a few more years to sort out that beneath all of this consternation was the deep knowing that the type of person my parents would approve of and the type of person I would approve of were not the same type of person.

Yet a life of singleness was out of the question, unless an angel from heaven alighted on the rooftop outside of my bedroom window with a message from God, declaring my heavenly Father wished me to dedicate my life to celibacy. Because God would never tell me to do something without also telling my earthly father the same thing, the angel would very shortly alight on my father's bedroom doorstep. Or another angel would be speaking to my father at the same time. Or, most likely, the angel would speak to my father first. The angel might never actually come to me at all.

Bottom line, I wasn't really allowed to consider a life of singleness without divine appointment.

BOYS

In the parking lot after class, Trey asked me to the junior-senior banquet for the upperclassmen of our homeschool group. I mumbled, "I'm not allowed to date." He slinked away, biology textbook tucked under his arm. I proceeded to the car, relieved I didn't have to do any further work to reject a boy.

My family's restrictions around our relationships with the opposite sex worked in my favor at this moment. Though my parents had never forbidden dating—forever or until a certain age—they did say we should not give away the water of our well to someone who would not be our spouse.

My father taught us we should not get attached emotionally until God spoke to us, revealing our future spouse in some divine way. He touted Proverbs 5:15–18 as biblical support for this stance:

Drink water from your own cistern,
And fresh water from your own well.
Should your springs overflow into the streets,
Streams of water in the public squares?
Let them be yours and yours alone,
And not for the stranger with you.
Let your fountain be blessed,
And rejoice in the wife of your youth.

I spent much of my adolescent years repenting in prayer whenever I had a crush on a boy. I'd beg God to take away the feelings so I could focus on God alone. Somehow, I was supposed to make the jump from inappropriate feelings to appropriate feelings after I received word from the Lord that it was okay to do so.

Deductive reasoning told me if I were going to accept Trey's invitation, I'd have to prove to my parents that Trey had potential for marriage. If I couldn't, they'd ask why we weren't just going as friends. Though the obvious reason was that I was a sophomore and wouldn't be allowed to go unless I went with a junior or a senior, doing the work to get approval for a one-night date in the company of our peers was using up precious permission points with my father. And, unfortunately, Trey wasn't worth it to me.

Permission points were arbitrary currency in the bank. I had to ask permission for almost anything social and had to be willing to justify the reason. There were certain folks who got an automatic yes. My friend Anne was one of them. Anne's parents were raising her in a similar fashion to the way my parents were raising me. Anne was also charming and good at talking to adults. My parents loved her.

But a boy I barely knew, who fell in the realm of acquaintance at best, wasn't worth the anxiety of asking. I wasn't attracted to him, and I knew he wouldn't be able to withstand the interrogation from my father that came along with any boys we brought into the house, whether we liked them or not.

A year earlier, I had met a guy named Jason at a camp that taught teenagers how to insert themselves in politics so Christians could eventually take over the government of the United States—yes, these camps exist, and this is their intention. Almost every kid who went was homeschooled. Jason was friendly and, bonus, wasn't afraid of me (boys and girls in these spaces always seemed to make one another nervous). We'd hung out a few times, and he was easy to talk to.

During one assembly, I arrived right before the program started and squeezed in a row that happened to be a few rows behind where Jason was sitting. Jason turned around and saw me. "What are you doing way back there?" He motioned to an empty seat in the row where he was sitting.

Instead of annoying my fellow mates in my row by squeezing past them to get to the aisle, I stood up on top of my chair and stepped onto a space on the chair in front of me. "You're amazing," Jason said, laughing. He reached his hand back and helped me step over the next row of chairs.

I don't remember any sparks of attraction with Jason. I do remember awareness that he was one of few boys in that space who wasn't afraid to touch me. We had easy conversation, something not always accessible between awkward teenagers who were socially and emotionally stunted through the isolation of homeschooling.

When camp was over, Jason called me at home a few times. I was fifteen, and this was before I had a cell phone. Our easy conversations continued over the phone.

Then one night, he called and my father answered. My father told him I wasn't available. Jason did not call again after that.

I think it might have been the first time a boy ever called the house to speak to one of Dad's daughters. Soon after, a new rule took formation in our midst: For boys who were friends, they still had to talk to our father. They had to commit to my father that they would only be friends with his daughters, and if that ever changed, they would speak to him first. My father said it was because he wanted to preserve the friendship. If my father told the poor sop no, then we could all continue being friends without emotional entanglement.

Yeah. Right.

I believe my father just wanted to control the friendship. I believe he didn't want any guy becoming more than friends without his knowledge or permission. Control in the name of protection. Because any boy who violated this rule, who dared to speak to a daughter about their feelings before they spoke to our father, was immediately cast out and their character came under attack.

I didn't know if any of these things would come to fruition when Trey asked me to the junior-senior banquet. I just knew a guy I wasn't actually interested in wasn't worth the anxiety of getting my father's permission. So I kept it simple by saying I wasn't allowed to date.

In my later teen years and early twenties, no guy seemed worth it. When I was twenty-four, I had a few flings and accompanied a couple blokes to events as their date. I never told my parents. If they'd ever asked or found out (which they never did), I would have told them I planned to handle my own affairs when it came to the people I ended up dating (though this open defiance would likely have ended badly, as any open defiance did).

I found out much later that a couple guys had followed the rules and asked my father if they could date me. He told them no, and I never knew about it. At least one of those guys just disappeared from my life, without explanation.

Preserve the friendship, my ass.

In my mid-twenties, I felt I couldn't trust my father. Even when I was still living with my parents, I was already quite determined that if I were ever going to get married, they would not have a say in my relationship. My sadness about this reality never superseded the clarity on this decision, because if my parents had access, they would intentionally try to sabotage it. I'd seen it happen too many times to hope for anything different.

MESSAGES

I have a group of friends who are all at various stages of making shifts in their faith. We all come from a variety of Christian traditions and denominations. Some still identify as Christian. Some do not. Some go to church regularly or work for a church. Some identify as Christian but don't want to participate in institutional church anymore. I call this group of friends The Renegades.

During one gathering, while we consumed charcute-rie, wine, and old-fashioneds, I asked them what messages they received in the church about marriage and gender.

Here are some things they said:

"You can't really talk about marriage or sex inside of evangelicalism without talking about gender. Everything is gendered in evangelicalism. Cisgender male and cisgender female. Heterosexual. There were no other categories." —Aurora

"Never say anything bad about your husband. Evangelicalism is extremely image-conscious." —Aurora

"You need to find a spiritual leader in a man. But this is not actually in the Bible." —Terri

"It felt sinful to stay in a dating relationship with someone I didn't think I could marry. He had to be a spiritual leader. If I couldn't see myself marrying them, I needed to break it off. It was sinful to keep dating them. Dating was for marriage only." —Terri

"I heard so many sermons on Ephesians 5 [the "marriage chapter" in the Bible]." —Aurora

"A woman's role was to respect her husband and have sex with him. Men were supposed to provide comfort, security, and protection." —Terri

"The obligation-sex message led to guilt when not wanting to have it." —Aurora
"I was told to stroke my husband's ego even if the sex is bad." —Jessica

"Had to have sex when you didn't want to. You feel guilty for not wanting to. I didn't want to have the conversation about why I didn't want to. My husband was conscious [of] when I didn't enjoy it, but I didn't want to talk about it because honestly I didn't know why I didn't want to have sex. So it definitely led to pretending I was enjoying it just so I could avoid having conversations." —Aurora

"The 'two shall become one' message promotes forced intimacy and enmeshment. Our marriage played out as egalitarian, even if we supported the complementarian stance outwardly." —Nancy

"I had experienced sexual abuse and sexual assault. But then when I got married, I surrendered so much of my autonomy and power to my husband. Because of the sexual abuse, I really needed bodily autonomy. But I didn't feel like I could have that or communicate that. It made me uncomfortable when my husband would stand behind me, but I didn't feel like I could tell him that. It made me uncomfortable when he'd stand in the doorway. I felt like I was being blocked in, but I thought it was my problem. I gave up so much of my power to my husband as soon as I got married. I was instantly aware of the power dynamic as soon as I got married." —Nancy

"As a pastor's wife, I was so programmed to support my husband's vocation and passion. This would've been so much different if he had been in a different vocation. But as a pastor's wife, I was free labor, the second pastor who didn't get paid." —Aurora

"Endless emotional labor. Constantly editing everything I say or do so that I am not overstepping or being unsubmissive." —Aurora

"During my bridal shower, one of my mother's friends told me it was my job to keep my husband satisfied sexually. My husband sexually abused me while we were dating and during the entirety of our marriage. Near the end, I worked really hard to only have sex

once a month, because that's how little I enjoyed it."
—Elaine

"Constantly felt like I needed to make my husband's life comfortable even though we were both working full-time." —Nancy

"I believed after I had sex before marriage that I could only marry the person who I had sex with because nobody else would want to marry me because I was damaged goods. Within one year of marriage, the sex was really bad." —Jessica

"I was emotionally immature and sheltered from home-schooling. I really needed therapy. I did not need to get married." —Jessica

"I felt relieved when I got married because someone chose me. I had to learn to find my worth, and just being me, outside of being married." —Terri
"Women are shamed for having an active sex drive."
—Stephanie
"I was told the physical nature of the penis and vagina fitting together is the proof for the created order and heterosexual sex." —Terri

"Most of the pressure for a good marriage is on the woman, but then some men who are not wired to be the dominant type feel a lot of pressure when they don't match up to the narrow standard of what it means to be a strong leader. A strong leader [in the church] means that the man makes the decisions." —Nancy

These beliefs are not isolated to a handful of fundamentalist spaces. While I received harmful messages about gender, gender hierarchy, and marriage from my family of origin, an extreme expression of Christian patriarchy, once I graduated from that cult into the world of evangelicalism, the messages weren't very different. Just more subtle.

My colleague Becky once told me she felt like the only reason she had a good marriage was because she got lucky, that evangelicalism had set her and her husband up for failure. I've come across many women in the spiritual abuse recovery world who have expressed the same sentiment.

Women are conditioned to be quiet and submissive. Men are conditioned to be dominant and controlling. Controlling men are considered good leaders. Men who are not controlling are considered weak. Assertive women are considered bitches and Jezebels. Quiet and mild women are considered ideal women.

I did not imagine this.

ALONE IS NOT ALONE

Carol's eyes were literally glistening as she talked about John and how much fun it was to be married to him and how he made her life so much better. She was raised up in her seat like a schoolgirl with a massive crush—only it was a mature sort of crush. The sort of crush that develops out of really difficult times. It's strong but mellow. It's vibrant but measured.

My friend Carol got divorced after five years of marriage. Those five years were very lonely and miserable, and after the divorce she was pretty sure she was never getting married again.

Then she met John, who was also divorced and pretty sure he wasn't getting married again. They'd both determined (separately, before they met) that the only way they'd ever marry again would be if the marriage was going to somehow make their life better. Otherwise, it wasn't worth it. Misery in marriage is one of the worst sorts of misery there is.

There we were, inside P.S. Kitchen in New York City, about to see *Some Like It Hot* before it left Broadway. She talked about how easy it was to talk to John and how they talked all the time. She told me about a Christmas gift he'd made her and she felt so seen and known. Then she said, "The happiest people are happy married people. Then happy single people. Then unhappy single people are happier than unhappy married people. Unhappy married people are the most unhappiest people."

I must concede, for Carol, this is true. She was miserable in her first marriage and extremely happy in her second marriage. But Carol, by her own admission, wasn't single for long. She got married very young to her first husband. Then she was only single for a couple years before she met John.

I will also concede that Carol knows what it's like to be both miserable in a marriage and extremely happy in a marriage. I will defer to Carol on this experience, considering I have never been married.

But I will defer to myself about singleness, and how, even though I have Carol's report and know that, if I ever have a partner, I want it to be like that—something that makes my life better—I didn't walk away from that conversation longing for Carol's life.

I am very happy that Carol is happy, and I don't want Carol to have my life, either. Because I don't think she'd be happy with my life. I also don't think I'd be happy with her life. It's something I know deep down in my bones. I just can't imagine that marriage would make me happier than I am right now. But I also know that if I choose marriage someday, I will choose something that will enrich my life. Otherwise, I can't see myself leaving my current life behind.

Carol's theory might be sound: that the happiest people are happy married people. I can imagine it's the only way to do it. I can also imagine a miserable marriage is just awful. Maybe it's the compounding factor of the second person. If you've got two people who are happy, you've got double the happiness. If you've got two people who are miserable, you've got double the misery.

But I've got to take a moment to push back on the two-person theory. And this is where the concept of marriage breaks down for me and I don't know I can fully agree with Carol's declaration.

I think most people have a view of marriage and singleness that is relatively binary. If you're single, they say, then you're alone. If you're married, you've got a partner. If these were the only two options, then yes, it makes sense most folks would choose marriage over being alone.

However, it's important to me that I make something very clear. As an expert single person with lots of experience at being happy and single: Being alone does not mean you are alone.

What do I mean by this? Well, let's take the trip to New York with Carol as an example. I didn't go to New York alone. I went with Carol. We had an amazing time. We built a memory together and shared an experience and lots of laughs. We saw three shows with original casts, and we'll never see those exact shows again. While John certainly enjoys theater, going to that many shows in that short of time isn't really his thing. So Carol enjoyed that with someone who wasn't her husband (something I really admire about her). She wasn't alone on that trip, either.

We both flew to New York separately, but that's a pretty normal human experience and definitely didn't feel lonely. My friend Katie picked me up from the airport, so I got to talk about the trip as soon as I got back.

This is a moment in which I sometimes miss having a partner: when I get home from an experience and want to share it with someone. But if I ever feel this way, I just call a friend (sometimes many friends) and I get a chance to share. Sometimes I write about it. I get to bask in the joy of this really amazing experience, and then I go about my life.

I didn't feel the lack of a partner for one moment during that trip. I never once thought, *Oh, I wish I had someone to share this with*. I *had* someone to share it with. And it was great!

As a single person, I don't just have one someone. I have many someones. I have different someones for different things. Carol is definitely my theater friend and might actually be more obsessed with theater than I am. She definitely knows a lot of nerdy facts that I just don't retain. I don't have many other friends who are *that* into theater.

Simultaneously, I don't mind going to shows alone. In fact, I rather enjoy it. Going to the theater by myself is one sort of experience. Going with another person is different, but it's not necessarily better. I enjoy both for different reasons. I know people who would never go to a show or a movie by themselves. On one hand, they are allowed to have their preferences. On the other, I feel like limiting yourself to experiences you have to share with a partner or a friend is—well limiting.

I like myself. I like being with myself. I like being myself with another person, but I don't need another person to enjoy being myself. I enjoy the company of others. I also enjoy my own company. I get to enjoy the best of all worlds. My life is broad and expansive and full of endless options and possibilities.

I think a lot of folks look at singleness and think, *That must be so lonely*. Sure. Loneliness is a common human emotion many of us feel. I feel lonely sometimes. But I think the loneliest of feelings is when you're surrounded by people and none of them understand you. They don't understand you because they don't want to know the real you. They'd rather you play the role they've cast you in and don't want to hear it if you say, "Hey, wait, that's not really me."

I've had this experience loads of times. You get this sickening, sinking feeling in the middle of your ribs, and it keeps sinking into your stomach over and over, like the mythological Sisyphus and his boulder, except you're not pushing the boulder up a hill, you're trying to keep it from rolling down into your stomach. It keeps going down until you stand up, shake it off, and get the hell out of that place. The most common place I've felt this sort of loneliness is when I'm with my family or former church people who don't know what to do with me because I'm not bound to a man through marriage.

Typically, they just ignore me, because all they can talk about is their children and I don't have any. It makes me want to stand on my chair and say, "Do you know how exciting the world is? Do you know how exciting my life is? There are so many things to talk about. So many subjects to explore! Your children are great, but we've been talking about them for three hours. Can I tell you about this amazing musical I just saw in New York? It's called *Merrily We Roll Along*. I got to see Jonathan Groff and Daniel Radcliffe perform in real time, and it was fantastic!"

But I don't feel comfortable voicing this because it might remind them that they chose to have children over other experiences, in many ways because of their religion. It might make them sad or jealous. Or they might really be limited in their ability to even hold space for other people's experiences because their family is so all-consuming. Or perhaps they think a play in New York is nothing compared to birthing and raising new life. They've determined their life is more important than mine.

So I don't usually push it. I don't try to make them see me. I certainly feel lonely in these moments, but the loneliness isn't because I'm single. It's because, in certain company, I'm not accepted because I'm single. This sort of loneliness is not my fault.

It's due to injustice in the world. It's because of the patriarchy assigning value to people based on their marital status.

I've felt lonelier in these moments than I did when I drove my car from Washington, D.C., to the West Coast. I was in my car, by myself, for six days straight. I was less alone during those six days than I have been in certain company.

I've learned so many things since my journey of researching spiritual abuse began. The marriage and gender hierarchies are the foundation of so much of the abuse. However, it's incredibly tricky to suggest this to people. For many of the folks who've dared to explore this further, it often leads to a full-on implosion of so many of their beliefs.

A lot of marriages don't survive the deconstruction process. The reasons are varied, but here are a few common ones: The male-identifying partner can't let go of the beliefs that give him power and soothe his insecurity; one or both members of the couple realize they don't actually want to be married to the other—or that they don't want to be married at all; the female-identifying member of the couple discovers the reason she is unhappy in her marriage is because she had to give up her entire identity, or she discovers she's in an abusive marriage. Many, many women (and perhaps men, too; I just haven't heard as many of them admit this) discover the only reason they got married in the first place was because they felt pressure from their community or they feared another offer would never come.

Many people stay in unhappy or abusive marriages for the same reasons they got married to begin with: economic, social, or religious pressure.

Sometimes people figure out a way to remove themselves from a toxic or abusive marriage, only to find themselves back in the exact same sort of relationship because they never addressed the theological toxicity that led to the first marriage.

I'm going to suggest a solution that I have rarely heard anyone share: *What if we all learned that being alone is not alone?* What if we expanded our view of intimacy? What if we gave ourselves more options for vibrant, fulfilling relationships than the singular option of joining ourselves to one other person for the rest of our lives? What if we explored the world, had adventures, deconstructed our beliefs, and followed our dreams with people who were for us, not because of our marital status but because they just liked us and wanted to be a part of our team?

What if there was so very much more to life than marriage? And what if, when we figured this out, we grew to like the variety of options? What if we grew to like ourselves by ourselves?

What if we learned to have fulfilling lives—married, partnered, or not?

I have a feeling the evangelical church would hate this—so much. But then again, it might trigger the End of Days and Jesus might come back. Since so many evangelicals are living for the return of Christ, maybe there's a chance we could all get on board with this.

NINE: BODIES

If They Control Your Body, They Control You

TATTOOS

I got a tattoo of a quill pen when I was thirty-two years old. I was living in D.C., and two of my former interns from youth ministry were visiting. These former interns had several tattoos apiece, so I figured they'd be the best people to get a tattoo with. I'd researched tattoo parlors and found one with quality ink and good reviews.

The spring snow swirled in the streets as I entered Tattoo Paradise with the image of my quill pen saved on my phone. I wanted the quill pen because I am a writer, but I'd also looked up the meaning of feathers because I figured a lot of people would think it was just a feather.

One meaning of a feather is freedom. When I discovered this, I immediately knew this was the tattoo for me. If I could characterize my life by anything, I would say my life is punctuated by a constant quest for freedom.

Initially, it was freedom from the clutches of my family system. I moved out of my parents' home when I was twenty-six years old, under the cover of darkness, and determined that even if I had to sleep in my car, I would never go back and live with them.

But this physical leaving did not fully equate to the freedom I so desperately sought. So much bondage exists in the aftermath—in the trauma we must heal from, sometimes all our lives. But as someone who is on the healing journey from trauma, one I anticipate will continue for years to come, I don't believe trauma itself has to be a barrier to a thriving life.

The first contact the needle made with my skin was shocking, like an instant intense sunburn. I hissed through clenched teeth and squeezed the hand of one of my companions. After that initial shock, the area where the needle drew the design slowly began to numb. I chatted with my friends and the tattoo artist. Then it was over. I walked out of the tattoo parlor into the snow, giggling and talking quickly as the endorphins continued to fire. I immediately wanted to get another one. This is why so many people keep getting tattoos, rarely stopping with just one: It feels so good.

Several years later, I returned to my hometown for the wedding of one of my sisters. In preparation for encountering unhealthy family members, my therapist and I came up with some grounding strategies. One of them was placing my fingers on my tattoo and reminding myself that I am free.

I still do this from time to time. Trauma can make you feel like you are trapped again. Like you're back in the place that once held you captive. Reminding myself that I am free now is also a reminder of how hard I fought to get where I am. I will not concede this ground willingly, though the same forces that once held me continue to demand submission.

I know a lot of people get tattoos after they leave high-control religion. It is a way to reclaim their body. Some churches and facets of Christianity consider tattoos sinful. Control comes in many forms, and someone telling you what you can and cannot put on your body is one of the most common signs you're starting to enter cult territory.

As we start healing from trauma, we cannot leave our bodies out. After all, the spiritually abusive communities didn't. They may have taught us to fear and hate our bodies, but that is because *they* feared our bodies and the role our bodies might play in gaining freedom, of telling us something was wrong.

One means of subterfuge is the revolution of our bodies. When high-control religion told us to rein our bodies in and make them submit to Christ, we can free our bodies by listening to them. Our bodies are a part of our humanity—they are us. To care for my body is to care for me. To trust my body is to trust myself. To give my body a voice is to acknowledge that what I have to say is important.

SKIRTS

When I was a senior in high school and for a few years after, my family became heavily involved in a religious organization called Vision Forum. It was a world those of us who've escaped now recognize as the Christian patriarchy movement or the stay-at-home-daughter movement. We became involved because my parents were searching for like-minded believers. (Translation: Christian-identifying people who did not think they were weird for not allowing their daughters to go to college.)

Vision Forum doesn't exist now. It disbanded after allegations that the leader, Doug Phillips, sexually abused his children's nanny.

I remember Doug Phillips as an extremely charming human. He gave me a lot of attention, I presumed, because I was the oldest girl who was boldly paving the way for my siblings (to a destination I couldn't begin to locate). He sent me a book in the mail that he inscribed. At twenty years old, when I started going by a different first name, switching from Katie to Katherine, he switched over without missing a beat. It was impressive.

Thinking about it now makes my skin crawl.

The organization was based in Texas, but they had conferences all over the country and internationally. At one of our first events, we walked into the auditorium in Boston on a blustery November evening and discovered we were one of the only families with women wearing pants. My sisters and I had made jokes before arriving, wondering if this was the sort of place where all the women wore skirts. But I don't think any of us expected to stand out quite so starkly.

I was proud to be one of the pant-wearers. I was proud to go out running in the mornings, knowing exercise wasn't something most of these women were accustomed to. I was even more proud when I left two days early from the conference, grabbing a taxi to the airport to jump on a plane back to my hometown because I had rehearsals for a production I was in. I desperately wanted everyone to know I had a life outside of them.

My sister Macey wore skirts most of the week. I didn't notice, but that first night in the auditorium, she disappeared back to our hotel room to change into a skirt that reached to her ankles. Later, she confessed that she'd felt out of place. I was surprised to learn she'd *changed* for these people. My brain could not compute. I just didn't understand the orientation to conform to people we barely knew.

I would learn, years later, that siblings will often have different experiences and reactions within the same context, due to any number of factors.

At future Vision Forum gatherings, my mother applied more and more pressure to wear skirts. My father was, strangely, silent on the subject. Either he didn't care or he let my mother do the work for him.

I was determined to only wear skirts I would wear anyway. There is nothing wrong with wearing a skirt. They can be fun and pretty. I had this really cute one that was denim and covered in gold lace and sequins. I'd found it at a vintage store. I wore wedges that tied up my ankles, making sure if I appeared to conform with the skirt, I'd be sure to stand out with the shoes.

However, I noticed some strange behavior in the men when we adjusted our wardrobe. Usually the men ignored us at these events. Most of them had trouble looking us in the eyes or even acknowledging our presence.

But then we put on skirts.

Suddenly, more men were looking us in the eyes. Smiling when they opened the door for us, wordlessly giving us their nods of approval.

It pissed me off.

At the same time, I learned the power of an extra few inches of fabric.

We stopped going to those events because, I think, my parents were disappointed at how few marriages were happening in that space. The single men seemed to be marrying women outside of the Vision Forum world, leaving behind dozens of spinsters who perpetually lived in their father's home. I think my parents were hoping to find husbands for us. When the odds weren't great, we moved on.

It was a sigh of relief. But I'll never forget those days or how the influence of those people contributed to the fortification of control in my family.

GOOD ENOUGH

My body was never quite good enough. I know this because recently I was looking at photos from the year I lived in D.C. I turned thirty-two in D.C., and I weighed 135 pounds in those photos. It was the skinniest I'd been since before moving to Mexico at twenty-eight. My commute to work involved nearly three miles of walking a day, easily forty-five minutes of aggressive city strolling, my workbag slung over my shoulder.

I didn't bother with a gym membership. I kept a couple kettle-bells and used online videos for a weekly session of weight lifting (because my personal-trainer sister said it was good for me). That was the extent of my exercise routine. I ate whatever I wanted, and I drank alcohol *a lot*.

I look at those photos and think, "Wow, I was so skinny! Look at those muscle indentions in my thighs!" But even then, I remember wanting to get rid of the thin layer of belly fat on my stomach that had shown up in my late twenties and never went away.

I can't even see that belly fat now. I don't know what I saw back then. From a photo perspective, my stomach is entirely flat. Yet at the height of what some might call my ideal body, I still found something to critique.

It's interesting to observe now how my body was never quite good enough. It's a metaphor for how I ultimately felt about myself: Never quite good enough. Never quite satisfied. Something could always be better. *I* could always be better. Do better. Always.

I've tried to remember if there has ever been a season where I was entirely at rest. Where I'd done enough and could just *be*.

I didn't start learning about the idea of being rather than doing until later on in life. I honestly think it was after I left the institutional church, when I started expanding my sources for knowledge outside of Christian books.

While in seminary, I found little oases of folks who talked about things like self-care and said things like "We are human beings, not human doings."

I'd always been a big Sabbath keeper. I think this was partly a necessity because I worked *hard*. I'd get to my day of rest and I would literally crash. I guarded that day with extreme fierceness and couldn't understand how other people didn't seem to need a day off. I worked so hard during the other six days; a day off became a break of survival.

It is only recently that I've learned to recognize that I feel like I need to earn my rest: that I have to kill myself for six days so that I am worthy of that day off.

The frenzy of achievement is embedded into Western culture. What the church did, however, is spiritualize this frenzy. I grew up surrounded by people who were always working, working, working. "Working for the Lord." They quoted verses such as Colossians 3:23–24, "Do your work heartily, as for the Lord" and "Whatever you do, work at it with all your heart[…]. It is the Lord Christ whom you are serving."

> *Make sure the kitchen is spotless after dinner. You are cleaning for the Lord.*
> *Study hard and get good grades. Your mind belongs to the Lord.*
> *Eat healthy. Work out. Your body is a temple for God.*
> *Be the first to the office and the last one to leave. You are representing your heavenly Father.*

All of these messages compounded into one: I did not belong to myself. I belonged to a deity. That deity got to use me however he chose, and it was my job to be an open and willing vessel of service.

For most of my life, I've felt like I had to earn my rest. It took great effort to bring myself to a place of equilibrium and truly believe the words I'll often say at the end of the day, "You've done enough today."

What ultimately shifted my relationship with my body was my study of trauma. The more I learned about my body's internal instinctive mechanisms for keeping me safe, the more in awe of my body I felt.

These internal mechanisms prompted me to dissociate during my years with my family. I shut down emotions that were unacceptable and shape-shifted in the presence of my abusers in order to keep them happy and keep their eyes off of me. I learned to adapt and blend in. I learned to be what I needed to be in order to survive.

My body worked so hard! "Way to go, body," I'll say these days. Lately, I've begun engaging my body in conversation, like it's a real person (it is). "How ya doing, body?" I'll check in on it periodically, just to make sure I'm paying attention.

After a rough season with the nonprofit I started after leaving the West Coast church, my body began to shut down. This led to serious conversations with my body. "Do you want to keep doing this?" I asked. "You've worked so hard. You've done so much. You've kept me safe my whole life. If you're ready to be done, if you're ready to move on, just let me know." I was willing to give up an organization I'd built from the ground up in order to care for my body. I'm learning to see rest as something my body deserves just for existing, not as something I need to earn by killing myself.

Exhaustion was once a sign I could take a break. Now, I just take a break. Exhaustion is no longer the norm. My body deserves good things.

I deserve good things.

PLEASURE

Even in near-poverty, I was willing to make sacrifices for my first love: theater.

During seminary, I lived on $900 a month. I remember praying before attending school, asking God to provide enough for me so I wouldn't struggle. I'd lived with the anxiety about money for almost a decade by then. I didn't want to be working, attending school, and constantly thinking about money.

As luck would have it, I rented a bedroom from an eighty-year-old woman for $80 a month. She didn't have internet, so I had to get a box that cost me $40 a month. My sister Joann helped me out by covering my cell phone bill while I was in school, and every semester, Nana sent me a $500 check.

I was on the Affordable Care Act, and that was probably the best health insurance I've ever had. I had a scholarship that covered 50 percent of my tuition, and I took out loans for the other 50 percent. I just didn't have it in me to kill myself the way I had for college. Additionally, where college was a means to an end, I wanted to enjoy seminary. Grad school was also more expensive.

A lot of our textbooks were available for rent from the library, so I avoided paying exorbitant fees for school books. I'm really glad I utilized the library, because any book I did purchase ended up getting sold or gifted a few years later.

I saw a handful of shows during my two years in St. Louis, most of them at The Muny, the city's outdoor theater that is known for having hundreds of free seats. (Side note: I think we should strive to always make theater accessible for those who can't afford it.)

A couple times, I dished out what was an exorbitant amount to see a show at The Fox.

The Fox Theatre is still one of my favorite theaters, topping The Pantages in LA and any Broadway or London theater I've ever been in. The first show I saw was *Wicked*. None of my seminary friends wanted to spend the money, so I went alone.

I took a roll of twenties to the box office on a Thursday night (Thursdays were my day off from youth ministry) and waited in line.

I got a ticket for $60, a seat with a minorly obstructed view. The energy of the crowd buoyed my excitement to see a show I'd been hearing about for years. I could feel the buzz from my pelvis up through my chest.

The buzz increased with each song, each line that brought collective laughter from the crowd. I had not known before watching that *Wicked* was about an outsider who gets a chance to become an insider but decides to turn it down because it would mean she'd have to suppress what she values: justice and equality. It's a story about friendship and chosen family. The male love interest ultimately chooses the outsider over the glitz and glam of the world on the inside, but the main love portrayed in the show is the love between Glinda (the good witch) and Elphaba (the wicked witch).

I resonated with Elphaba's words in the song "Defying Gravity" that say love you are always fearful of losing isn't love at all.

Wicked is about being misunderstood. It's about pursuing dreams. It's about sacrificing dreams for the sake of your conscience. It's about suffering and overcoming and fighting for what you believe in.

As the cast bowed at the end of the show and I got to my feet for the ovation, I could feel my entire body vibrating. My skin tingled all over as I joined the crowd flowing toward the exit.

I experienced a powerful desire to make out with someone.

When I got to my car, I giggled like someone intoxicated. I wondered if this was what an orgasm felt like. I have only ever felt a similar orgasmic pleasure in the presence of other art.

Today, as an accomplished Orgasm-er, I can compare two different types of orgasm. An orgasm prompted by clitoral stimulation prompts a more physical response. An artistic orgasm—brought on by the presence of theater, a gorgeous painting, or perhaps a concert—is more emotional for me. I feel both very deeply in my body, and the sensation, in my opinion, is more fantastic than any inebriation or high. It's a high on its own level, and it's what people call pleasure.

Sex is not the only or ultimate form of pleasure. Folks who only think of sex when they hear the word *pleasure* may have a limited perspective of pleasure outside of sex.

If you seek to control others, pleasure is dangerous. People who are alive and vibrating are less likely to tolerate totalitarian control. There is a reason the same cultures that seek to control sex also seek to control art.

If there is ever a time in the future when I can no longer have sex or an orgasm is unattainable, I think I will be okay. My options for pleasure are wide and varied.

I had an artistic orgasm before I had a clitoral one. Both are intoxicating, but the high from an artistic orgasm lasts much longer.

I think an artistic orgasm might be more difficult to access. Not everyone will be able to have this experience, as art isn't everyone's stimulant. With sex, it's possible to go through the motions (though not ideal). But I imagine there are other forms of orgasmic pleasure. Athletes talk about a runner's high, and I wonder if this is something similar. Some foods can stimulate pleasure as our taste palates are brought to the edge and released into ecstasy.

Part of embracing our full humanity includes searching for pleasure and expanding what pleasure can be. Pleasure is embodied, involving the senses. I recommend starting with anything that will activate at least two senses. Experiences of pleasure will likely result in stars behind our eyes and gasps from deep inside. There is no limit on where we can find pleasure.

The high experienced in the theater that night was combustible, but I'd accessed similar sensations before. I remember feelings of energy from a writer's high when I was working on stories in my bedroom on the top floor of my parents' home. I remember voraciously reading certain books that caused me to forget about the world, consuming me in the present moment of the story.

I remember feelings that resembled happiness. Somehow, art allowed me to breathe life into a till-then unnurtured creature of joy. This wasn't the sort of joy my parents seemed to demand we display for our family and for the outside world—a false happiness that led to exhaustion and confusion. A joy that ignored pain and other uncomfortable parts of humanity.

I stumbled upon this true joy when I first saw children's theater performances with Nana, who bought season tickets for us until we were too old to go. I stumbled upon joy the first time I was cast in a tiny role in a community theater production. I stumbled upon it when I set my alarm for 6 a.m. and powered up my ten-pound laptop, spilling black and white letters onto a document that would eventually become my first novel.

I don't believe we can experience the full spectrum of joy until we are fully in our bodies and attuned to our true selves. I don't believe we can be fully attuned to our true selves until we acknowledge and accept our desires—even, and especially, the ones culture tells us we're not allowed to have.

And this is why high-control spaces want to control our bodies. If they control our bodies, they control us. We find our freedom when we reclaim our bodies and give those bodies pleasure and every good thing they deserve—just for being human.

TEN: HUMANITY

How to Be Human

SUBHUMAN

In a humanities class in graduate school, I learned that when most women look in the mirror, they see a woman first and a human second. When most men look in the mirror, they see a human and almost never consider their gender.

According to this class, the reason for this difference in perspective between men and women is because men have socially and historically been viewed as the ideal human and women have socially and historically been presented as the leftovers.

You could say the second chapter of Genesis, when Eve was created, supports this belief.

I specifically remember this part of grad school because I cannot imagine thinking of my humanity without my gender. My gender is intricately woven into my identity and, as far as I know, always has been.

From the moment I was born, my parents socialized me as a girl. My mother wasn't what you would call a girly girl. She played sports, enjoyed camping more than my father did, and only put ribbons in my hair for family photos. But I knew when I grew up I would be a woman. I would have children (somehow; I had not yet learned the mechanics). I would primarily be responsible for the home and the meals and the grocery shopping. I'd nurse babies from my breasts (that would one day grow in), and when the babies got a bit older, I'd teach them from a schoolroom that was once a dining room converted into a space for child-sized desks, with posters of human anatomy hung on the wall.

And a globe. My classroom would have a globe of the world.

Never once, as far as my memory serves me, did I wish I were not a girl. Even when I grew into that anticipated woman and experienced heavy burdens and extreme barriers because of my gender, I never wanted to be a man.

I wanted to be me. I wanted to be considered a full, legitimate human being, worthy of dignity and respect and opportunities. I didn't want my gender to change so I could do more. I wanted the world to change so my gender was no longer a problem. I like being a woman. And if someone mistrusts me, denies me access, overlooks me, or mistreats me because of my gender, I consider them the problem, even if the surrounding systems deny the issue.

Why did I see this so clearly, even at a young age? My parents certainly did not teach me this, as they'd cemented themselves into the mold of gender roles like the concrete foundation of a house. If they didn't have gender roles (and by association, gender hierarchies), they didn't have a marriage. They didn't have children.

Long before I experienced gender discrimination in the workplace, in academia, in the church, my parents placed these shackles upon me and named it the freedom of God's calling on my life. They promised if I abided by God's purpose for me—to be a wife and mom—the rest of life would fall into place. I would be happy. My life would be blessed. My dreams would come true.

I really had no reason to think differently and not trust my parents. But a little piece of my soul always felt like something was wrong. How did I know? Some part of me kept that door of possibility open a crack. I believe I found freedom for two reasons.

The first is by sheer accident my mother birthed an artist when I was born. Artists, by nature, see the world through a unique lens. Many artists have an uncanny ability to see the future. We aren't all psychics (though some of us are). We are simply so in tune with the nature of human beings that we can see where the choices of humanity will lead. The irony that I am both a woman and an artist is not lost on me, for both have been mistrusted throughout history. Both have been considered sub-citizens. Both have generally had their voices suppressed.

The second reason I found freedom was the direct impact of other people. People who came along at just the right time to say something pivotal that stuck with me and penetrated the haze of brainwashing. People who helped me in practical ways, by loaning me a car or giving me a temporary place to live. People who showed me what love looked like and demonstrated that trust in a relationship goes both ways.

For better or worse, I knew if I stayed on the path my parents said God had chosen for me, I would shrivel into nothingness. For better or worse, I envisioned a future for myself that was far different than the one option they'd presented to me. For better or worse, I dared to believe my humanity mattered, which meant (and this is a dirty thought where I come from) my desires mattered. Even if those desires did not line up with the establishment.

One element of recovery from spiritual abuse is the fight to embrace our full humanity (and the rights that come with it). Indeed, this conversation is not divorced from the conversation about abuse. For someone to abuse someone else, to exert power over someone to cause them harm, they must have already determined the other person's worth. The abuser behaves in an inhuman way. By the abuse they inflict upon another, they strip away the dignity the other human deserves.

In my family, I was socialized as a female. Though they never said it explicitly, I was socialized as a subhuman. The messages from my family cult are powerful—like the creeping destruction of Mordor spreading over Middle Earth, sucking life from animals, plants, and creatures. It takes time and intentionality to push back the shadows so live things can grow freely. It takes time and intentionality to embrace our full humanity—and everything that comes with it.

NEVER GOING BACK

After I left the abusive West Coast church, I planned to go back to full-time ministry. I even told my new boss in the corporate world that I did not plan to stay in that job very long. At the time, I was already in the interview process with several churches.

The denomination of churches where I'd heretofore made my career believed the Bible said men and women were equal—they just had different roles. I determined this environment was no longer for me and I would only seriously consider churches that had female pastors and elders.

One of these egalitarian churches invited me out for a weekend-long interview process. The business of the church interview can be extremely intense. They care far more about your beliefs and your knowledge of the Bible than they care about your ability to do the job. (It might be that they believe if you are thinking the right things and have the right knowledge, all the other things will fall into place.)

During this interview weekend, I saw immediate red flags. At the first welcome dinner, one of the men on the search committee for the position I was interview-ing for shared loudly how obnoxious he thought a certain brand was. He displayed his ignorance by failing to notice I was wearing two items of clothing from that same brand.

It wasn't that he ridiculed a brand I happened to like; it was that the church had chosen someone like him—a bombastic, arrogant idiot—to be on the committee. He was the opposite of a good impression.

I noticed a handful of other potential concerns by the time I arrived at the lunch prior to the big interview the following day. Church interview weekends are full of touring, individual meetings, and experiences. Typically, there's one intense interview session that either consists of a bunch of individual interviews or one big one where you undergo an inquest by a committee. This church planned a committee-style interview and hosted a lunch with the committee and me so we could get to know one another in a casual setting before the big moment.

During the lunch, the male-dominated committee talked about sports for about three-quarters of the time. The one female committee member (who was on the opposite side of the table from me) told me later she was inwardly cringing that they'd consumed the time meant for them to get to know me by talking sports, when I clearly wasn't participating in the conversation.

I think that was when I knew. For all the church's bravado and claims to care for women (one of the pastors had scoffed when I'd told him women weren't allowed to be pastors at my old church), the men actually didn't behave much differently toward women than the men in the patriarchal churches I'd previously worked for.

I was there to interview for a significant position they claimed to really want to fill with a woman. Yet they proceeded to talk over me and ignore me at a lunch intended *for* me.

Throughout the weekend, I spotted more red flags. During the actual interview, the bombastic, arrogant idiot asked me how many people I had led to Christ. I replied that I believed in a more relational approach to ministry, but the fact that anyone was keeping a tally struck me as a glaring warning sign.

The final red flag was the last breakfast before I left for the airport to fly back home.

One of the concerns I'd picked up on was that the three previous people who'd filled the position I was interviewing for had seemed to leave their post in quick succession. The last person had only stayed for a year. The committee communicated the rapid departures were due to some flaw on the side of the employees, which immediately tipped me off that there was definitely more to the story.

I got the rest of the story from the staff who'd worked directly with these (apparently) recalcitrant former employees. I'd specifically asked to meet with members of the team who would be working under me if I accepted the role. My former experience taught me they could be my greatest allies if I worked there. I also knew from experience that churches often ignore the thoughts and feelings of lower-level staff, and I wanted to start out from a place of letting those staff know I valued their experience.

I remember their faces as they leaned toward me across the diner booth table. Over a breakfast of eggs and bacon, in voices barely above a whisper, they told me the prior staff members had been pushed out. The most recent departure, it seemed, had been the most difficult. I could tell these team members were hurt and sad. Their story revealed they had a good reason to be.

When I discovered the three prior employees who'd filled the position before me had all been men, it made me wonder if the committee was specifically looking for a woman because they thought she'd be easier to control.

I would never know for certain. A couple days after returning home, I called the recruiter who'd connected me to the church and declined the position.

Not long after, I decided my career in full-time ministry was over.
But that final church interview circuit, consisting of at least a dozen different churches all over the U.S., had certainly confirmed for me a suspicion I'd been trying to ignore: There was something wrong with the evangelical church—and it went far deeper than opposing views of men's and women's roles.

CONSENT

Freedom of religion is a fundamental human right. People have a right to believe what they want to believe. But can we draw the line where those beliefs lead to violating the human rights of others?

I think we can.

My father believed (and led me to believe) that the labor I contributed to the family paid for my room and board: construction work on the house (every Saturday, most holidays, and some weekdays), watching my siblings, tutoring my siblings, grocery shopping, meal planning, and cooking for my family (for a while I was the primary cook for our family of nine). This labor was my way of compensating him for having my own bedroom, access to the family lake house, the occasional "gift" of $100, and some pretty extravagant vacations (none of which I asked for). This labor was also an apprenticeship meant to prepare me for my (er… his?) chosen career, that of being a wife and mother.

However, even as an adult, within this arrangement, I wasn't free. I wasn't free to make all my decisions for my life. I wasn't free to go where I wanted when I wanted. I wasn't free to date who I wanted (or date at all). I did not have negotiating power to change this arrangement, increase my "pay," or end the arrangement. I didn't have an HR department with whom I could log complaints when I believed I was being mistreated.

I wasn't free to believe what I wanted.

Under these circumstances, one might venture to say I was a slave, a word I don't use lightly. One might say my father's beliefs crossed a very important line: that of violating my human rights.

How do we define human rights? What does that mean? What does it look like?

It's more than equality, because the very word suggests something we are equalizing. Like women are equal to men (men are the standard) or Black people are equal to white people (white people are the standard) or transgender people are equal to straight cisgender people (straight cisgender people are the standard).

It's more than a belief that all humans deserve to be treated with respect based on the truth that all humans have dignity. Most people would agree to this. The question then becomes, what does respect look like? What does it mean to have worth and dignity—simply because of our humanness?

In my experience, a few power holders (usually men) get to decide what a human right is. If they decide that respect for women means protecting women, then as long as they are keeping women out of physical danger, they have done their job and women should be happy. If a woman decides the world should be safe enough for her to walk alone at night—so she does—she's held responsible when she's assaulted because she was outside of the protection of a man.

If men decide that respect for women means providing for them, then as long as they bring home a steady paycheck, they have done their job. If a woman decides she wants to work, she's disrespected herself (and her husband) by taking away his opportunity to show respect.

But the very reality that a man mistakenly believes he gets to determine what respect looks like for a woman suggests that the man's definition of respect—and therefore his beliefs and opinions—are superior to the woman's. In all the church systems I was a part of, I believe every man I worked with would enthusiastically declare he respects women. They would die on that sword.

The thing is, they rarely asked the women. When they did, most women didn't know any different and agreed that the men in those spaces treated them with respect. I know I sometimes agreed out of fear of hurting the male power holders' feelings if I suggested that I'd like to be treated differently. Most of the women who protested their treatment (including myself) made little headway and eventually left.

The preconceived definition of respect was deeply embedded into most of the women in that system. In every instance I can recall, the male-dominated system determined what respect looked like. The women were conditioned to acquiesce—because the system often claimed this definition of respect came directly from the Holy One.

This stuff is personal. It's why it leads to so much chaos and fear and abuse whenever it's challenged.

I believe I have a fundamental human right to decide what respect looks like to me. Because my opinion and beliefs are important—because my desires matter based on the simple fact that I am human—I get to decide what my dignity and worth look like.

I have the autonomous choice to say, "I feel disrespected." If the person (or system) I am speaking to does not listen, then I have the freedom to extricate myself from the system, relationship, or situation. Or I have the freedom to fight back.

I have done both with varying results.

While living in my parents' home, I struggled in my early twenties with my lack of choices and freedom. I once spoke to Micah about this. He was in the military at the time and no longer living at home. I tried to describe what I wanted: "I'm an adult. I should be treated like an adult."

"That's good, that's good," he affirmed. "Tell Dad that you want to have the same freedom as Mom."

It was a starting place, but I remembered thinking that I didn't want to be treated like my mother, either. I really wanted to be treated with respect. And I was starting to piece together the truth: It seemed my father didn't treat anyone with respect, least of all his wife and children.

At the same time, he appeared to vehemently believe he loved and respected us because he provided a large home, expensive vacations, and basic resources. What more could anyone want?

Something that helped me shape my idea of respect—of human rights—came from the principle of consent. This term generally shows up in sexual situations, but I think it has wider implications. For example, if my friend offers me a gift, she is consenting to pay for the gift and I am consenting to receive it. I get to decide on what terms I receive that gift (no strings attached, or else it's not a gift). My friend gets to decide on what terms she gives the gift—how much she spends, what it is, and when she gives it. If neither party freely consents, then the gift is not given or received.

This opens the question of what happens when someone does not or cannot give consent. As a mental health professional, I am a mandated reporter. I am required to report if someone is causing harm to a minor, elderly, or disabled person.

In a sexual situation, a minor is considered by law as unable to give consent to sex. In some states, it is illegal for a member of the clergy to expect sexual consent from a congregant, even if they are an adult, because of the power differential. (I hope this becomes more common as we understand power dynamics in sexual situations.)

It is my belief that if a gender hierarchy exists in a marriage, then a wife is never fully consenting to sexual relations with her husband. If a gender hierarchy exists, a man's sexual relationship with his wife can easily creep into the realm of abuse.

High-control religion is intrinsically anti-consent. Most communities are conditioned to believe they have the answer for the whole world: a relationship with Jesus. The underlying assumption is that evangelicals know what is best for others; therefore, others do not know what is best for themselves. Evangelicals place themselves in situations that allow them to offer this answer. Sometimes it is not an offer; rather, it's an aggressive ad campaign that compels people to accept by inciting intense emotions. Like fear. If we can get people to fear hell, then folks will convert. If we can convince people their problems will go away if they submit their life to Christ, then many souls will relinquish their autonomy out of desperation.

It begs the question if they are actually converting of their own free will or if they are merely responding to emotional manipulation.

What is humanness? It's a question that lies at the foundation of many cultural shifts. Of wars. Of laws. It's an important question because it determines who is treated well and who is not.

Adolf Hitler legitimized mass genocide by convincing a nation that a number of different people groups (including queer people and Jews) were subhuman. The United Kingdom and the United States made slaves out of one race by convincing those with lighter skin that they were superior to those with darker skin.

This then brings up questions of gender and race as aspects of our humanity. How we have historically defined gender, race, and sexuality is also determined by the power holders. They need these traditional definitions to exist so they can categorize us and decide what respect looks like for us based on our placement on the human scale.

Most wouldn't say we aren't human. They just might say we aren't human enough to own land. Or to vote. Or to have custody of our children. Or to maintain control of our financial resources when we get married. They might grant a husband the authority to confine his wife to a mental institution based on his word alone. They might value the word of a man who adamantly claimed he did not rape a woman over the woman who said he did—because the system decided men are more trustworthy than women.

This stuff is personal to me because I have been on the receiving end of mistreatment based on my gender for most of my life. But most of the power holders would not define it as mistreatment. Because of my gender, in their eyes, I received all I was owed.

Entire worldwide committees have formed to determine what basic human rights each person deserves and to enforce the equitable treatment of marginalized groups. I believe it's important to mention in a book about spiritual abuse that yes, people have a right to the freedom of religion, but religion—specifically the high-control version of Christianity—has often subdued and erased the rights of people in the name of God.

Some people inside Christianity are conditioned to believe they do not have rights, or if they do, they must surrender those rights to God. Some, like myself growing into adulthood inside my family, never learned they had rights at all.

For the time being, I have concluded that to be human means I get to have a say in what dignity and respect mean to me. I get to decide that I deserve choice, chance, and opportunities. I get to speak up when my conditions are not met. I get to write articles and books when I believe something needs to change. I get to remove myself from institutions and relationships that are unwilling or unable to acquiesce to the life I have chosen.

I get to have desires. I get to believe those desires are good. I get to pursue those desires.

I get to choose.

ELEVEN: SELF

Nice to Meet Me

FLEE OR DIE

After she left a cult she'd been in for many years, a colleague of mine told me when she would go to a restaurant, she'd order the first thing on the menu that sounded good. This simple exercise started to teach her how to trust her instincts again. It helped her recognize that what she wanted was a good thing.

One thing that is important for healing on the other side of spiritual abuse (of any sort of abuse) is regaining a sense of self. What do we like? How do we feel about the state of the world? Our jobs? Our neighbors? Our friends?

What do we want out of life? What do we want right now?

When you are abused, someone uses their power to take away your power. One of the abuser's methods is to erode your sense of self. The abuser takes away your desires and replaces them with their own. They take away your values by telling you what you should value instead. They reward you for agreeing with them and punish you for disagreeing with them.

With spiritual abuse, they tell you what God thinks of you. They orchestrate what your relationship with God should look like. They say *should* a lot. Like "You should be praying constantly throughout the day" or "You should be reading the Bible every day."

There's nothing inherently wrong with reading your Bible or praying, but by telling you how you're supposed to interact with these intimate spiritual practices, they're taking away your agency, your ability to have a relationship with God that is personal. They think they know you, God, and what God expects better than you do. Then, to really make you mistrust yourself, they tell you that you should be humble by deferring to them and other people on all matters in life. They praise you when you don't trust yourself and call you selfish and arrogant when you make a decision without their blessing.

Getting a sense of self back—like my colleague ordering what she wants at a restaurant—is one of the first steps to breaking free. Most people start this process while they are in the abusive environment or relationship. It's what helps them recognize that maybe what their leader, or abusive partner, or controlling parent is telling them isn't entirely true. Once that little crack of doubt enters, they can start the process of questioning things. Usually this begins inside their mind, or with little alarms that go off in their gut.

By my teens, I'd read the entire Bible a couple times. I started to notice some stories and themes my father never mentioned. I started to notice inconsistencies and contradictions. They aren't hard to find.

My father was very dogmatic about making sure we ordered our lives according to scripture, so one day I asked him, "What if you and I come to different conclusions about what the Bible is saying?" (My implied question was "Which of our viewpoints wins when we are both using the Bible to justify our choices?") He didn't give me an answer in words. But his face contorted into what I interpreted as confusion. It was like he couldn't fathom that any rational human being would ever come to alternate conclusions about the Bible.

Years later, I learned in seminary that there are hundreds of perspectives on the Bible. Dozens and dozens of interpretations. And hundreds of denominations based on these differing perspectives. My father either didn't know or didn't care.

I was in my early twenties when many of the dynamics of my family of origin converged, and I knew something was really wrong. I'd had an inkling for some time, but the incident of getting kicked out of my parents' home when I was twenty-four years old helped me see that I wasn't going to change things while I remained inside the system.

I felt like I had two options: Comply and shrivel up and die. Or leave.

EXPLORING

In my thirties, I starting teaching myself how to date. After my family of origin and the church royally damaged this area of my life with harmful teachings, I began addressing the impact of these messages while learning how to interact with the opposite sex in the context of a date.

Most people start learning how to have romantic relationships when they are in middle school. To begin this process as a fully formed adult leads to lots of faking confidence and internet searches for things like "questions to ask on a first date."

While learning how to date, I was also investigating the depths of my own desires. Did I even want to get married? I'd been so conditioned to believe marriage was a certainty—almost a requirement—to be a godly woman, I never really got the chance to explore if it was something I even wanted.

Around the time I arrived in D.C., a year before I moved to the West Coast, I began to wonder if there was something inside me blocking me from getting married. This was after grad school. I had just turned thirty-one.

A coworker gave me the materials from a course she took about clearing away everything that prevents you from realizing your dreams. It was an embodied workshop on how to manifest your desires.

I finished the course, complete with an altar I prayed over. The altar contained a voided check with the salary I wanted at my next job written on the back. It contained a mug with the word *Work* on it, which symbolized my desires for my dream job.

It also contained a book with one of my favorite love stories (*The Return of the King*, which tells Éowyn and Faramir's love story). This book symbolized my prayers for my future mate.

Even then, my prayers for money and career were more fervent than my prayers for a husband. I could visualize my desires for my career. I could not visualize the sort of person I wanted for a partner.

Part of me thought it might be because I'd never met a real human being who got close to representing what I wanted. The only people who resembled what I wanted were characters in stories. But even before I'd ever met or known another author, I could visualize a life as a writer. I began to create it in real life and imagine what that future might look like.

I believe I actually was blocked about marriage: I wasn't that interested. But having little or no desire to get married was so culturally unusual, it took me into my mid-thirties to embrace it.

It seemed *everyone* wanted to get married and pursued dating with this end in mind.

I knew I wasn't like my peers. Dating was an intellectual exercise and something I did for experience. I was a scientist doing research on a foreign species. (Me? Or the guys I dated? I really couldn't say.) When I'd come home from a date and friends or roommates would ask me how it went, I saw the light in their eyes, hoping for a dramatic ending or a good story that promised future dates.

I almost always had a good story. I almost never went on a second date.

After somewhere around a hundred dates with different people, I got to the point where I actually enjoyed dating. I liked getting to know new people in that context. I also typically got to explore a new restaurant or go to a show with another person, rather than going by myself.

Sometimes I'd complete a date and enthusiastically talk about how much fun I had.

My audience usually leaned forward eagerly, waiting for the announcement I'd be seeing the bloke again. They were always confused when I said no. They didn't understand how a good time on a date did not constitute a second date.

I've only been on one date where I found the guy extremely physically attractive. He was the only guy I ever really wanted to go out with a second time.

He was the only guy who outright rejected me with a text, indicating he didn't see us going anywhere. He was a Christian who was clearly looking for a wife.

But God, he was hot.

I've gone on a second or third date with a few other people, but only because I made a bet with myself to see if I could take it to the next level. One of these guys was someone who was moderately attractive and interesting. He was a successful screenwriter, and I found all his stories about Hollywood fascinating.

We met on a dating app while I was living on the West Coast. While we were on the first date, I told myself that I was going to take us to the second date.

I'll admit I was playing a character with a goal in mind when we made plans to go out again.

On the second date, we went to a rooftop bar. The night air was perfectly tepid, and the stars shown clear in the sky. It was very romantic.

We took glasses of wine outside to the pool deck and sat on lounge chairs by the hot tub. We weren't there for long when a very drunk couple waddled out in bathrobes. They shed their robes and descended swimsuit-clad into the whirlpool at our feet.

Then they proceeded to have intercourse, right there in the hot tub.

My date and I looked at each other, silently consulting on whether we should move. With our eyes, we decided we were there first, so we continued talking while our fellow guests continued humping.

Later, after he walked me back to my car, I was relaxed and giddy from the wine and the entertaining bonding experience, so when he hugged me, I lingered.

And lingered.

I got the impression he wanted to kiss me.

I can't explain why I lingered quite so long.

After I was in my car with the door shut, I muttered, "Shit." Turning down a third date would be difficult after that lingering hug.

He was going to Comic-Con in San Diego the next week, so it would be at least a whole week before we would hang out again.

He texted often over the next several days.

I was aware I was only responding to his texts, never initiating.

I was aware I was fighting annoyance and calculating how long I could wait in between responses without being rude.

I told a coworker about it. I said I wasn't enjoying texting and I wasn't excited about the next date. She confirmed it was a sign I wasn't interested.

For our third date, we grabbed coffee. He brought me a bag full of paraphernalia from Comic-Con. My heart sank at his excitement to tell me about his time in San Diego.

I knew he had hopes for us that I didn't share.

I didn't know how to let him down easy. We weren't a couple, but it *was* a third date. I owed him clarity, but instead I pretended everything was fine for the duration of our time together.

When I got home, I was exhausted from faking enthusiasm.

I am ashamed to admit I didn't end things in a courageous or kind way. I just stopped replying to his texts.

If I could do it over, I would be more forthright. I would close the door in a more gracious way.

I don't regret not going out again, but it's weird how after three dates, I sort of missed him. I don't believe I should have kept things going with someone I wasn't excited about, but I got a small taste of companionship,

> of what it would be like to have a partner who was
> excited to see you and tell you about their day.
> This might be why some people get married.

BASELINE

How do you reconnect with yourself when you never had a sense of self to begin with?

It can be very difficult to find yourself when you don't have a state of equilibrium to return to. If you have a clear sense of *before the abuse* and *after the abuse*, you know what baseline feels like. You have some barometer for when you're on track.

But this can present its own set of challenges as you realize that you can't really go back to the way things were before. While you can reintegrate with your intuition and definitely learn how to trust yourself again, you have a sense of being permanently altered. You can't go back, and this can cause a lot of sadness and frustration. It can feel like you've had years of your life stolen from you, and this isn't far from the truth.

Finding a sense of self for the first time can be overwhelming. You look back on the choices you've made throughout your life and wonder how many decisions you made because you truly wanted to make them. Or did you just make those decisions because that's the choice you were conditioned to make?

After I left my family of origin, when I moved to a different country, I chose a career path within a church denomination that was complementarian, which presumed equality of the sexes, but equality with different roles. Men were supposed to be the spiritual leaders of the home, and only men could be elders and pastors in the church.

I think about this choice now, and I know that I would have been extremely uncomfortable in a denomination that believed in equality of the sexes with no exceptions. I was more comfortable with a denomination that resembled the world I'd left. I had no idea it was comfortable because I'd been conditioned to believe this was God's way. I had no idea I'd gone from one version of patriarchal control into a slightly less extreme version in the church.

While I sometimes wonder if that choice was made for me, I know, deep down, that I made this choice because I *was* trusting myself. I didn't feel comfortable throwing everything away. I had affection for the Bible and for God, and I wanted to teach the Bible in a way that was engaging and kind. I thought the Bible was a fascinating story, and I felt like most of the teaching I'd experienced growing up had been bullying. I wanted to share what I saw with other people. I wanted to help people. I didn't fully agree with the teaching in my churches that women weren't allowed to be pastors, but I didn't think it was that important. As long as I could do the work I wanted to do, I didn't care about the job title.

I made the best decision I could with the knowledge and resources I had at the time. I would certainly make a different decision now, but I'm ten years further down the road than I was when I made the original choice. I grew as a person. I learned things. Today, I'm making the best decisions I can with the knowledge and resources that I have right now.

And this, in essence, is what it means to trust yourself. It's doing the best you can. It's making mistakes and learning from them. It's learning to look at the past with honesty, to grieve the sad things and appreciate the good things. It's learning to live in the present and listen to the self that is you in the here and now. It's learning to let the future take care of itself.

TWELVE: SEX

The Church's Obsession

CLARITY

I don't remember the specifics of what led my friend Amelia to issue the statement "The Bible is clear," but she said the words in response to something I said, referencing specifically that the Bible was clear sex should only happen inside of marriage between a man and woman.

I was on the phone with her on a fall evening, enjoying the lovely cool night air and the gas-burning fireplace on the patio of my apartment complex, a year or so after moving back to the Midwest from the West Coast.

Because the bulk of what we were talking about had nothing to do with sex, and her statement was in response to something I'd said as an aside, I let the comment go and might have even changed the subject, as I often did when we stumbled into a realm we could no longer discuss.

This was happening more and more often since I'd left the church. Since the institution was no longer my place of employment, I had the freedom to ask questions and seek answers about things that had always bothered me. Sex was one of those issues, though I didn't feel like I entirely changed my views in the years following church work. I felt like I was finally free to explore and be open about what I think I always believed deep down.

While I attended and worked for the church, I wasn't having sex. But I knew a lot of unmarried people who were. Some of those people volunteered in the youth ministry. Technically, I should have fired them for being sexually active, as it was against the rules of the church for a volunteer to have sex outside of marriage. For some reason, I didn't see how their sex life had anything to do with their ability to mentor teenagers. For some reason, I didn't see how their sex life had any bearing on whether they were a decent human being or not. I say "for some reason" because I swam in the waters containing the message that sex outside of marriage was one of the worst sins. Ever. If you were having sex outside of marriage, there was a very good chance you weren't a Christian.

But I had a lot of friends who had this kind of sex and still seemed to love Jesus a lot. They were kind and good people. My brain could not grasp that sex was enough to alter them completely. However, I can't explain why I thought this way. This wasn't how I was raised.

So after I left the church, I had more freedom to explore what I really thought about sex and sexuality. I discovered I never really had a problem with sex outside of marriage and did not think that the Bible was very clear on that subject at all.

I'd always been in conservative churches that declared sex was only for marriage and true marriage was only ever between one man and one woman. I knew my job would be on the line if I ever dared to issue a counterstatement (or suggest a counterstatement), so I just never made it a point of contention. I wasn't like my peers, with personal stakes in the game. I didn't have the same interest in sex as almost everyone I knew.

Once my phone call with Amelia ended, I stayed on the patio and continued to stare into the fireplace, flames flickering as I noodled on her "the Bible is clear" statement.

It's interesting to think I felt like she didn't really know me, considering all we had been through. She was a longtime friend from the long-ago time of living with my family and being under my parents' control. She'd had her own journey of waking up and breaking free; most of it occurred when she got married.

When I was going through the excruciating experience of navigating the abusive West Coast church, we talked on the phone almost every day. She is still one of the most empathetic people I know. She helped me survive that season just like she'd helped me survive my family. When I wrote my mother the letter to give her boundaries, Amelia read the letter before I sent it. When my mother responded two months later, I forwarded the email to Amelia first. Then we got on the phone and Amelia read it to me so I wouldn't have to be alone while I encountered my mother's words.

I loved my friendship with Amelia, but I'd grown increasingly concerned that if I were honest about what I really thought about things (mainly sex and the church), she would withdraw. I would lose her. But I realized the only reason I defaulted to her belief system was the same reason I defaulted to the belief system of the church. I feared rejection. Sex didn't seem worth the price I'd have to pay to be open about my beliefs.

But this wasn't about sex. It was about the belief that "the Bible is clear." If I continued to interact with Amelia, I needed her to know that we were not operating out of the same paradigm. Our beliefs did not have the same foundation. I needed to let Amelia see who I really was.

A couple days later, I called her again. I started by saying, "I need to let you know how statements like 'the Bible is clear' land for me. I don't think the Bible is clear on a lot of things, but it's the statement itself that bothers me. It's a conversation shutter-downer. Once you say it, you close the door on discussion." I then went on to explain that it bothered me she would say it to *me* of all people. I had a seminary degree and had taught the Bible for nearly a decade. If anyone had a right to make that statement, it was me. But I wasn't making it because it just wasn't true.

I continued, "People who say the Bible is clear typically want to believe one of two things: If someone arrives at a different conclusion than they do, they want to be able to dismiss that person as ignorant. Or they want to dismiss them as someone who is outright rejecting the Bible. I'm neither of those people. I'm not ignorant. I am also not dismissing the Bible. It has a lot to offer, but I don't think it's clear. On a lot of things."

As the conversation ended, I felt like I'd gotten my point across. I wanted to bring my beliefs into the room and stop defaulting to Amelia's beliefs just because it was easier. Yet as the conversation drew to a close, Amelia said, "I will try to remember that the Bible is painful for you and try not to say things like 'the Bible is clear.'"

My heart sank, but I was too tired to push back on this. It felt like she hadn't heard me at all. Rather, her paradigm caused her to place me in a whole new category: I wasn't rejecting the Bible. Nor was I ignorant. Now I was being dismissed because I was traumatized.

It is true that I have experienced being shamed, belittled, coerced, and manipulated with the Bible. For nearly two years after leaving the overtly abusive West Coast church, I found the Bible painful. But even as I recover from the trauma of experiencing abuse in the name of God and the Bible, I am aware the source is not always the Bible itself.

For some people, the Bible's supposed clearness is a lifeline. If they don't have the clarity of the Bible, then they have lost certainty in almost everything. I know this because I used to be one of these people. Even though I admit, there were so many things in the Bible that didn't seem to make sense and didn't add up, from the very first time I read it through cover to cover at the age of fourteen. Because I found it confusing, I assumed for most of my life that

I was just stupid. All the spiritual leaders around me kept saying, "The Bible is clear." The problem must be mine.

Even after I went to seminary, I only walked away with more questions. But I couldn't ask those questions while I was inside the institutional church. I couldn't ask those questions while the church paid my salary.

Not really, anyway.

ORGASMS

I was in my thirties when I learned what a clitoris is. From the internet. The first few times I engaged in solo sex, I inserted my fingers inside myself and mimicked sexual encounters from movies. Nothing happened. I thought I might be doing it wrong or wasn't properly aroused. (I prefer the term *solo sex* to *masturbation*. Masturbation has hard syllables. Solo sex is softer and embodies how I see it: as a full and complete sexual experience.)

Many survivors of purity culture experience shame the first time they engage in solo sex. I did not have this experience. This was likely because I was already on the journey of realizing there was something off about what I had been told about partnered sex, masturbation, and sexuality.

I asked a friend how she felt about masturbation, and she told me it was a part of her sexual encounters with her husband. She'd spend a good long while getting herself warmed up before her partner joined her in the process. She used to engage in solo sex as a single person as a form of rebellion against God for not giving her a husband. I admired her literal spin on telling God, "Fuck you."

Even then, we did not discuss mechanics. A few months later, I heard the word *clit* as a passing comment and trembled when I entered the word into a search engine. This led me to a book by Laurie Mintz, *Becoming Cliterate*, which I added to my electronic holds list at the library (there was no way I was checking out the hard copy for all the world to see).

The book has a whole chapter with exercises on ways to masturbate. The next time I tried solo sex, I blocked out an entire afternoon. I did a long yoga session to relax my body and mind. I turned on a Latin playlist (music I'd noticed assisted in turning on my loins). Then I read a sex scene out of a Julia Quinn novel. Properly in the mood, I spent a half hour or so with the exercises from *Becoming Cliterate*. I didn't know what to expect from an orgasm, but I was pretty sure I didn't have one that first time around.

My next encounter, I introduced a thumb-sized vibrator from a starter kit I'd purchased, along with some lube. The orgasm was like a shock of electricity jolting through my body. I specifically remember the tingling in my toes. I laughed with glee that I *did it*.

Still unsure I was doing it right, I watched YouTube videos and Gwyneth Paltrow's *Goop* series on Netflix. The spasming, screaming orgasms we see on TV are just one sort of orgasm that can happen sometimes. It's not the ideal. It's also not typical. For women and other vulva owners, orgasm rarely comes through intercourse alone. (For many, intercourse isn't needed at all.) This is how our bodies work. We are not defective or subhuman. My journey with solo sex, with clitoral stimulation alone, was interesting enough for me to continue pursuing it and trying things out. It's meditative and one more way to be in my body. It's a part of my self-care routine. It's fun.

It was through this journey of sexual discovery that I realized that not only had the powers that be withheld information from me—they had also deliberately lied.

MUSICAL INTERLUDE

Scene I
*Lights dim on an empty stage. Spotlight on a woman in
regular street clothes.*
Cue music: "Maybe I Shouldn't Do This"

Maybe I shouldn't do this
I really want to *do* this
I really shouldn't do this
I really want to do this!

My head's definitely saying no?
Or is it?
My body's definitely saying go?
Or is it?
A lot of feelings
All at the same time!

Mom would say,
When in doubt, leave it out
My friends would say,
Just try it out

So many sayings
So many slogans
So many opinions

What is my opinion?
What do I think?
How do I feel?
Can I do this if I don't know what I feel?

What's wrong with pleasure?
Why is pleasure so bad?
Why is it so dangerous?
Why are we so terrified?

Is it God in my head?
Or just—a lie?
Is my desire so bad?
Is my longing wrong?

He's hot, he's hot,
He's really, really hot
I want to jump his bones
I want to suck his mouth
I want his body on my body
And his hands on my ass
And my hands on his
Oh I want him
I really want him
I want him so much

Sex before marriage
Would get you labeled a whore
But it's hard to think of that
When I have tingling in my pelvic floor

I want this.
This. This moment.
I want this. It's mine.
No one's but mine.
It's mine. It's mine. It's mine.

Fade to black

Scene II

Spotlight on stage left. Same woman in a bed.
Upper body fully clothed. Lower body covered
by a sheet.
Cue music: "Just a Beginning"

I feel nothing
Absolutely nothing
I thought I might
Feel something
But I feel nothing
Not guilt, not shame
Not conflict, not pain
No blame
Just
Nothing

Am I numb?
No, I just don't feel anything
Or I guess I just don't feel wrong
Is that surprising?
Very, very surprising?
Am I surprised by how little I feel?

I don't think I'm in love with him
I'm not in love with him
Is it important I'm in love with him?
How important is love?
What even is love?

[Spoken] Ha, I know one thing for sure: I'm
overthinking.
Over- and overthinking. How do I feel?

This could be more
So much more
I want more
So much more

I want to feel fire
I want to feel love
I want to feel precious
I want to feel loved

I have power
I have a choice
I have reason
I have a voice

I can say yes, I can say no
I can say stop, I can say go
I can change my mind

I can give my heart away
To anyone I want
And I can take it back
Whenever I want

This is just the beginning
A very rough beginning
A messy,
Unremarkable beginning
A beginning

Just a beginning
This is my beginning

Fade to black

KNOWLEDGE IS POWER

My first messages about sex came from watching my mother carry four children. I don't remember the birth of Joann because she is only two years younger than I am. But I remember the others. I remember the swelling of my mother's belly. I remember the horror of discovering from Micah that babies don't come out of the belly button. They come out of the same place pee comes out, he said. I thought he was making it up, but how could someone make up something so awful? Also, how would a baby's head fit through there? It sounded so painful.

One fateful night when I was around six years old, I overheard the word *sex* while we were driving in the car as a family (perhaps an exchange between my mother and father). I asked, "What's sex?" and my perpetually sensitive and compassionate older brother busted out laughing. My father chastised him. Then my father kept me up later one night to show me some encyclopedia images and give me a scientific lesson, slowly building to the climactic revelation that sex was when a man puts his penis inside a woman's vagina.

My reaction was to scrunch up my face and declare, "That's gross." This was after I asked for clarification on the definition of penis.

My father said some other things about divine design and creation and beauty, but I don't remember much of that. I do remember him saying, "It's fun." This was probably the first time I ever doubted my father. How could that be *fun*?

It is my opinion that the whole idea of giving children "the talk" lends to this message about sex that it's something other. Special. On an altar of its own. What if we talked about sex and sexuality like we talk about the reasons we eat a balanced meal? That it's good for you. It's part of our body's development, and it is just as normal as our elbows or our kneecaps? Many modern sexologists and sex educators affirm this approach, but I know the reason why I was both kept ignorant and lied to about sex.

As an adult, when I started learning things about sex and my own sexuality, I started to feel a lot of things. First, I was so angry that I was in my *thirties* when I understood how much pleasure I was capable of creating for myself, but this knowledge had been denied me because of systemic deception in an effort to control women's bodies.

Second, I was in awe that my body had an organ dedicated to my pleasure. (Seriously, that is the clitoris's only purpose.) Plus, this organ is on the outside, easily accessible by me and me alone.

The powers that be don't want me to know this because if I have this knowledge, there is a chance I won't want or need a man. There is a chance I won't want or need marriage. As long as they perpetuate the lie that sex is only holy within a marriage between a man and a woman, and when you have sex within this context it is always amazing, then I have a pretty massive motivation to get married. Compound this lie about sex with the lie that divorce is the worst sin ever, and you trap a lot of unsuspecting people in marriage and give them a horrible sex life as the cherry on top.

To round it all off, in most of the cultures where this lie is perpetuated, they also believe men are the head of the home and the church. Ultimately, keeping women ignorant about sex and shaming them when they look for answers are part of an attempt to maintain control of women and keep men on top (in more ways than one).

If I have knowledge about sex and my sexuality, I know what I want and I have expectations for a partner. Or I have the knowledge and experience to decide I don't want a partner. This knowledge is powerful. If I expect a good sex life and my partner isn't interested in doing their work to contribute to our mutual pleasure, then I might go somewhere else.

I have the testimonies of at least a dozen friends, colleagues, and clients who have said if they'd had sex before marriage, they would not have married their partner. Sex reveals a lot about what someone believes about themselves. In partnered sex, you can find out a lot about someone, and the institutions of church don't want women to know what most men in these spaces are really like. If women are aware and believe they deserve better, they might start making demands. Or divorcing their husbands. Or—heaven forbid—refusing to get married.

You see, whenever someone is deliberately withholding information from you and shaming you when you ask questions or look for answers, odds are high that power is at the heart of it.

My married friends were just as ignorant about sex as I was, even after they got married. I am convinced of this because when they get divorced and start their journey of discovering who they are and what they want, I am the one teaching *them* about sex.

Also, my father's description of sex was inaccurate. What he described is called intercourse. Limiting sex to intercourse is a patriarchal, heteronormative view of sex, because intercourse is usually the most pleasurable for a man. Intercourse is not the most pleasurable for most women, because the clitoris is on the outside—part of the vulva (not the vagina). Intimate sexual experiences can be so much more than the reduced performance of penetration.

But they don't teach you that in church.

THEORIES

The church is obsessed with sex. It's the axis on which much abuse in the church spins.

I grew up believing sex outside of marriage was one of the worst sins ever. But why?

I have three theories. First, sex outside of marriage is relatively easy to regulate. If you do violate this mandate, it's a relatively easy sin to hide. Upholding this moral standard (or the appearance of it) makes it very simple to set yourself up as a good person. It also makes it easy to draw a line in the sand between the good people and the bad people so we know who is in and who is out.

Second, it maintains a system for marriage that traps women and emboldens and frees men. Most of the risk in premarital sex is on the woman, and women are the ones who suffer most when this transgression is discovered. Throughout the ages, even the most progressive societies have a more charitable view of men who have multiple sexual partners, while women are held to higher standards. In the most conservative cultures, women are supposed to be virgins (never having had penetrative sex) until their wedding night. In the fundamentalist world I grew up in, my friends and I assumed it was too much to expect the men we married would be virgins. As strict as the teaching was about staying pure, we all gave a grace pass to the men.

Current research suggests the happiest men are married men and the happiest women are single and child-free. I find this statistic sad but generally true. Marriage benefits men while it can be a detriment to women, even in today's modern society that has equipped women with far more freedom than we've ever had before.

My third theory is this: Shame around sex keeps abuse victims quiet, especially if they don't know it is abuse. How many pastors have claimed they had an "affair" with a parishioner when the power dynamic most certainly categorized the relationship as abusive? How many minors stayed quiet about the abuse they experienced because they were terrified of the repercussions of having sex? How many abusers use the church's stance on sex to deliberately manipulate and silence their victims?

Abusers are attracted to the church because of this belief system. It allows them to hide in plain sight. When the abusers gain positions of power, they perpetuate this belief system because it makes their proclivities easier.

Shame around sex creates a culture of silence. It creates a culture of ignorance. It prevents education about consent, leaving many people open and vulnerable to abuse.

System-regulated sex is very different from individuals establishing their own values around sex and sexuality. And a person can't establish their own values if they don't have accurate, healthy information. Systems that regulate the act of sex also seem to regulate the information. How many good Christians have been traumatized on their wedding night because they and their partner had no idea what they were doing?

The teaching on sex is dogma that can and has become abusive in the evangelical church. This teaching highlights how abuse isn't just an action or an inaction. Sometimes it comes from a theological viewpoint that is deeply embedded into the system: that a pure marriage between a man and woman represents the full image of God to the world.

The patriarchal leadership of evangelicalism needs this viewpoint in order to maintain power. The root of all abuse is the exploitation of power. This teaching is a deeply damaging and abusive position of power.

All in the name of obeying God.

THIRTEEN: APOLOGIES

When You Say Sorry (But Don't Mean It)

COERCION

In my family of origin, Steven Hassan's BITE model for coercive control is a helpful framework. BITE stands for Behavior control, Information control, Thought control, and Emotional control. But what makes all this control spiritual abuse is the reality that it happened in the name of God, using the Bible for support. It happened at the hands of an authority figure who claimed to speak for and hear from God.

The summer before my father kicked me out of the house, he coerced an apology from me. He only resorted to coercion in this incident because it was the first time I didn't apologize immediately the moment he corrected me. It was the first time I truly, deeply believed I hadn't done anything wrong—I had nothing to apologize for.

The reality that I would habitually apologize within a moment is evidence of the deeply embedded emotion and thought control of my family. If my father said I was wrong, I was wrong. Even if I didn't think I was wrong, I'd come up with some way to convince him that I believed his assessment. I'd make something up to appease him.

Then one time, I refused. It was so very clear to me that my father was wrong about me.

We were at the lake house my parents bought when I was nineteen. My father had just taken the boat out. We always had a designated cell phone on the dock whenever someone went out on the water. A few minutes after he left, that phone rang and Elizabeth answered it. My younger sister's face immediately went white, and she handed the phone to me.

Before I could get the phone to my ear, I could hear my father yelling. Through the rant, I deduced he'd arrived on the lake, ready to ski, and discovered there were no life jackets. He was furious at whoever had forgotten to put them in the boat, and the person taking the brunt of his fury was whoever was on the end of the line, who happened to be me.

Once I figured out what he wanted, I said, "Okay, I got it" and hung up. Little did I know this infraction would replace the life jackets in the seat of his rage.

When he returned to the docks, the life jackets were forgotten. He heaved himself out of the boat and onto the dock and began assailing me with verbal barbs directed at my disrespect, my negligence, my stubbornness. He wanted an immediate apology, and I desperately wanted him to go away.

However, something inside of me was confident I hadn't done anything wrong. I had enough self-preservation skills to not say, "I hung up on you because you were yelling." Instead I said, "I hung up because I understood what you wanted."

My answer did not appease. I was still guilty of disrespect and negligence and stubbornness (and probably a few other character flaws).

I could have ended the whole episode with a simple, fearful apology. For whatever reason, I decided not to apologize for something I did not think was wrong.

This resulted in his restricting me from using any of the cars. At twenty-four years old, I didn't own a car, and I didn't have a job. Despite the injustice, the cars were his, and with very few options for coercing me into behavior he deemed appropriate, he hit me where it hurt the most, making sure to add, "And none of your sisters are allowed to drive you, either."

The standoff lasted a week. During that time, Macey came back for a few days from working on the ranch we'd both worked at the summer before. Because she was not home when the incident occurred, we all assumed she didn't fall under the driver ban. My best friend also picked me up and drove me a few times. Nobody told me to apologize and just move on, but I could feel the unspoken influence I had to end this. "Just say you're sorry" resounded in my head, but at that point, I wasn't even sure that's what he wanted anymore. I felt, deep down, he was angry I was thinking for myself. He wanted to humiliate me, remind me he had all the power.

Unfortunately, I didn't have a plan for what would happen if this went on forever. All I knew was my father could be wrong. I could be right. And I did not have to believe I was wrong just because he said I was.

In the end, I told him I was sorry for hanging up on him. Disregarding the disrespect he showed me by yelling over the phone about a problem I didn't cause, he asked me if I thought hanging up was disrespectful. "Yes," I said. He was satisfied. I was relieved he didn't push me further, make me wallow and beg and write an essay of apology (a particular form of punishment he'd invented when I was a teenager).

This was the situation that caused me to realize I'd never be free of my father's cycles of rage until I had my independence. I needed a job. I needed to buy a car. I needed a college degree. And I needed to get out.

THAT F-WORD

People sometimes ask me, "Have your parents ever apologized?" I've always found this question strange—if I say yes, what does that mean? Does it mean I have to stop writing about my experience? Am I expected to engage in relationship with them? And, when it comes to a situation of abuse, does it even matter?

I think it's a strange question. Because the answer is, actually, yes. And no.

A year or so after my father kicked me out of his home for taking a job without his permission, I was once again living in his house, under the assumption of a tentative truce.

I was in my room, door open, and my father appeared in the doorway. He placed his hands on either side of the doorframe and said, "I don't ever think I've said it, but kicking you out of the house was the wrong way to handle things." He paused.

I waited.

"Do you forgive me?" His lip jutted out in puppy-dog fashion.

"Yes, yes, I forgive you," I said.

He nodded his head in one sharp motion. He departed, and I fled my room, heading down the hallway in the opposite direction.

I have a confession to make: I did not forgive him. I said what I needed to say to extricate myself from a terrifying situation. I felt he barricaded me in my room. His stance, full build consuming the doorway, hands braced against the frame Samson-style: It was a power posture. He'd trapped me with his body. That wasn't a request for forgiveness. It was a demand. You could say he attempted to coerce the forgiveness from me the same way he sought to coerce an apology after the incident with the life jackets.

An apology or forgiveness offered under duress, under threat, is not an apology or forgiveness. It's survival.

Notice also that my father did not say he was wrong. He said kicking me out was the wrong way to handle things. Implied meaning: He didn't get the results he wanted.

My father taught me his beliefs about forgiveness and apologies. He taught me that if you forgive someone, then the slate is wiped clean. You can no longer use that against them.

I don't believe my father meant to apologize. I believe he meant to force me into a situation where I could no longer use the experience of kicking me out of the house against him. I believe he wanted to take care of his end of things so any relationship problems would then be entirely my fault. If anyone ever asked *him* if he'd done his part to reconcile, if they asked him if he'd ever apologized, he could now say yes without blinking.

Nearly a decade later, I did actually forgive my father. But forgiveness never came until I fully acknowledged the magnitude of the damage my father had caused. Almost simultaneously, I severed my relationship with my father. Forgiveness came hand in hand with a severed relationship. They don't teach you *that* method of forgiveness in church.

How can I call it forgiveness if I no longer speak to my father? Because I no longer bear the weight of any responsibility for his actions. I have released him to bear the consequence. I am no longer responsible to save him, to help him, to hold him accountable. My forgiveness was for me, at the time I was ready. I experienced the release that people often describe after forgiveness. I felt free.

I believe if my father ever really understood the magnitude of what he had done, he wouldn't ask me to forgive him. He'd ask me to stay far away from him. He'd understand he was dangerous. He'd know that the absolute best thing for me is for him to not be a part of my life. He wouldn't try to text me or email me, especially after I ended our relationship.

Honestly, I think if my father ever truly repented, I'd know. Even if I were thousands of miles away, I'd know, because the foundations of the earth would shatter.

Any faux apologies up until now do not count. The attempt to both coerce an apology and coerce forgiveness were prime examples of spiritual abuse.

Forgiveness and apologies are the most spiritualized forms of abuse in Christian communities. My father's methods are acceptable because an entire system is designed to treat forgiveness and apologies like a formula. A transactional exchange. The system ignores complexities of relationships. It ignores dynamics of power. It doesn't have a category for abuse. Survivors of abuse often experience more abuse in the aftermath when the system pressures them to forgive, to engage their abuser in relationship without their consent. "Forgive as God has forgiven you," they say. But they leave out a lot of layers that apparently led to God's version of forgiveness—like torture, murder, and crucifixion.

APOLOGIES

My male therapist (the only one I ever had), the therapist who introduced me to box breathing and other exercises to regulate my trauma responses, bore witness to another healing moment, another episode seared into my memory.

Binary thinking, the idea that there are only two options and everything in life falls into one or the other, can be a result of trauma—a survival response to keep us safe. Everything in life is either safe or unsafe. There is no in-between.

We often learn binary thinking in evangelicalism. Such as, there are only two genders: man and woman. Only two roles within marriage: husband (spiritual leader) and wife (support system and caregiver). There is right and there is wrong—very little room for personal preference and the art of choice. It's biblical or unbiblical. People are either Christian or non-Christian. Saved or unsaved. Binary thinking is one reason I believe the church is formed out of the trauma its leaders have likewise experienced and have failed to recognize.

The first thing folks who leave must work through is the ability to hold multiple truths together. We must learn to sit in ambiguity and uncertainty. We must become comfortable walking through life without all the answers.

As a survivor, I struggled with this myself. For my survival, men in particular became binaries or categories of safe and unsafe. The only exception I made was for those I didn't know well enough to categorize.

Most men fell into the unsafe category for one reason or another. I still believe most men are unsafe, though I no longer believe they are all being unsafe on purpose. I believe they received a conditioning that was different than the conditioning I received as a woman, and they are merely behaving in accordance with their programming.

While this belief allows me to have compassion for men, I still hold them responsible. Here is my admonition to men, a famous quote attributed to the sage Maya Angelou: "Do the best you can until you know better. Then when you know better, do better." That's my final word on that.

I went straight to a therapy session after another meeting with a church person. This person was my boss Steve.

Remember the coworker the elder brought up at the Panera Bread? The one I was having conflict with? Well, several months earlier, at the beginning of the school year, my boss had turned the youth ministry over to me and this Veritable Ass. But I heard about it through my coworker, not my boss. We'd already been working together for almost a year, and that was plenty of time to pick up on the fact that this coworker did not actually like youth ministry.

Though it was already obvious, over coffee one day, he told me he didn't like youth ministry. He said, "This is just a job to get through seminary."

I believed this was problematic to running the ministry and I took my concerns to Steve. But the decision had already been made, and Steve more or less dismissed me. While I did not express this to Steve at the time, I believed he should have put me in charge. I had more experience than my coworker, actually liked teenagers, and was good at youth ministry. Steve even told me he expected my coworker to handle the bigger-picture, vision-casting part of the ministry and I would handle the relational part. He was fully aware my coworker was not relational.

Not relational in *youth ministry*. It's one of the most relational forms of ministry there is.

But of course, the unspoken reason that I was not put in charge was that I am not a man. If I'd been a man, they likely would have offered me a full-time contract with benefits. As it was, my coworker and I led the ministry together, and it was nothing short of a disaster.

The next few months consisted of my coworker running the ministry into the ground, parents expressing wariness at the state of things, students coming to me telling me they hated my coworker, and me scrambling to maintain relationships with students and parents that my coworker was offhandedly destroying. The following spring, Steve fired the Veritable Ass.

I barely had time to gloat in the aftermath of sweet, sweet justice when Steve asked to meet with me to discuss what the youth ministry would look like moving forward.

In a coffee shop near the seminary campus, he started the meeting expressing concern for my workload now that my coworker was gone. He didn't want me to take on too much. I thanked Steve for his concern, but internally I was relieved my coworker was out of the picture. He had never really done much actual work to begin with, other than showing up to Sunday school with an extremely dry sermon he'd already presented in seminary class that week. The relief of not having to clean up the Veritable Ass's mess would afford me more energy and more time to fill in any gaps that might be left behind.

Then Steve confessed something that surprised me. "He should never have been in that job to begin with. You knew that last summer. I should have listened to you. I'd love to give you the opportunity to share how you're feeling now."

Wait—was Steve apologizing *to me?*

As Steve invited me to express how I was feeling, tears began constricting the back of my throat. I held them back as best I could as I poured out the frustrations from the past year. Steve was an active listener, maintaining eye contact and nodding his understanding. He didn't interrupt me or correct me or try to justify any of his decisions. He said he was sorry. He asked me what I needed. I came up with a plan to keep the ministry going for the rest of the school year, and he agreed to it.

I was still dazed from the experience when I showed up at therapy. As I blubbered out what happened, I watched my therapist's face light up. "How do you feel now about your safe and unsafe boxes for men?" he asked.

Wide-eyed and stupefied, I said Steve didn't belong in either box. He hadn't belonged in either box to begin with. He'd done unsafe things. He'd hurt me. But he wasn't an unsafe person.

Steve had apologized for sidelining and silencing me. But his apology didn't end there. Over the next few months, Steve deferred to me on almost everything. But he didn't just passively agree to my ideas; he enthusiastically championed them, often taking the role of support system (a nearly unheard-of role for men in these church spaces). He was quick to say "Ask Katherine" when someone came to him with questions about the youth ministry. He asked me to come to staff and leadership meetings and encouraged me to give the updates.

Until this experience with Steve, I'd never in my life had a man genuinely apologize to me. On top of that, anything that looked like an apology had been laced with manipulation. Not only had I never received a genuine apology, any "I'm sorry's" were another weapon in my father's toolbox of control. He occasionally said "I'm sorry" in a way that seemed to indicate he was trying to prove to himself he was a good father and to wipe the slate clean. I wasn't allowed to be hurt after he said "I'm sorry." I had to pretend what he'd done had never happened.

Steve's apology was different. His words were just the beginning. He didn't expect me to behave as if his dismissal hadn't happened, just because he'd apologized for it. And he spent the next four months, before I moved to D.C. for another job, showing me he meant what he said.

That spring, I worked thirty hours a week for the youth ministry, attended seminary full-time, worked as a teaching assistant for a seminary class, and trained for and ran a 10K. I was exhausted, but the pure elation of no longer being held back gave me the energy to keep going.

I had so much energy because I was finally supported and encouraged in my passion. I had a boss who trusted me and championed me. I had a boss—even if it was just for a short time—who took responsibility for their mistakes. I had a boss who removed barriers out of my way and gave me space to soar. If that isn't an apology, I'm not sure what is.

FOURTEEN: TRAUMAVERSARIES

Stories in Our Bones

AUGUST

The Dementors in the *Harry Potter* series capture how I would describe my experiences with depression. The creation of these dark creatures that suck the souls out of criminals came out of J.K. Rowling's own experience with depression.

All the happiness has gone out of the world. I will never be happy again.

I am able to trace my waves of depression back to trauma triggers, especially what I call traumaversaries. August was always a particularly horrible month in our family. I believe my father had his own traumaversary in August—possibly related to his own traumatic upbringing—because this month he was always angrier than usual, and we spent the end of almost every summer grounded from activities.

I say it was August. Some of my sisters remember it being October. Perhaps it was both.

August and October became new traumaversaries for me when I lived on the West Coast. August was the month I realized I needed to leave the church, but I couldn't resign just yet. I was a single woman without the support of extended family. I'd moved for the job I was now planning to leave. I had only been there a couple years, so I did not yet have a plan B.

But the stress of working in an abusive environment while job hunting became too much for my body. I started getting a migraine every day, and my stomach was so upset I threw up almost every morning. By the time I reached October, I ended up having to take medical leave from work. My body recorded these new memories in the cycle of my year, so the following years, depression and grief would float to the surface during these two months, replaying the recordings of fear and confusion from my parents' home, as well as the betrayal and mistreatment of my toxic work environment.

These emotions weren't entirely inexplicable. They usually came with an onslaught of memories of things my father said and did or memories of being sidelined and silenced in the church job.

Traumatic memories are complex, those stored in our consciousness and those stored in our bones. Time doesn't erase all wounds. Trauma needs special care or it just sits in our marrow, waiting for activation. Like malaria.

So I set out to reclaim these months. My first book, a novel called *Hartfords*, released in the autumn, and I planned a book tour to all the cities where I once lived. The tour ended in New York City and D.C. during the month of October.

I know it rained when I was in New York, but that whole trip is in my memory surrounded by the bright light of the sun. I saw a show on Broadway with some friends, and it was the first time I'd been in the theater since COVID. I was interviewed on a podcast. It was my first studio interview, and it was really cool. So many of my former friends and acquaintances in D.C. came to my book event there. That trip was laughter and friendship and celebration for my beloved creation entering the world for the first time.

Residual traumatic memories will still arise in October, but the memories of a tour and the new life of my book compete for space in my psyche. I continue to intentionally add new, good memories to this month, making October *my* October.

A year after the book release, in anticipation of the potential August traumaversary, I decided to take a month off from Tears of Eden, the nonprofit I'd founded. I'd also planned an eleven-day dream vacation to Scotland with my friend Samantha as a way of taking back the month.

I was already in burnout. I could feel the signs closing in. I'd just moved into a new apartment. I worked full-time, ran a nonprofit full-time, and was in school again. At the beginning of August, I turned in my final portfolio of assignments for class and prepared to have some fun and rest.

I did not prepare for a disgruntled volunteer who began raising concerns she felt were dire.

If her concerns had been founded, they might have been alarming, but they were not urgent. I was disheartened as she attempted to take over my August, the August I'd planned for rest and recuperation. I did my best to listen to her concerns but ended up having to call an extra therapy session just before I left for Scotland so I wouldn't take the stress she was creating with me on my trip.

This was not how I wanted my August to go.

They say only sticks and stones can hurt you, that words roll off and make no impact. I believe we've proven the falsity of this cliché as we grow in our understanding of things like emotional abuse. A person can injure you, possibly enough to impact your whole life, without ever laying a finger on you.

More than personal injury, the volunteer's consistent pattern of behavior revealed she was no longer a good fit to work with the organization.

So in November, the board called a meeting. We asked her to take a break for a year. We had the meeting over video call, but I could still see the whites of her eyes as she sputtered with rage.

Sometimes you don't know someone is unhealthy until you create boundaries. That's when their true colors show.

The meeting ended badly. For two weeks she sent emails laced with barbs of manipulation, jabs at me that were unfounded—a last stand in an attempt to maintain control.

Just after Thanksgiving, my body officially shut down, coinciding with the anniversary of the date I officially resigned from the abusive church. I noticed it the first Saturday in December, after helping my friend Martha and her son set up their Christmas tree. When I got home that evening, I could barely walk straight. I took a bath to try to help me relax and struggled to climb in and out of the tub.

The following Monday, I went to the doctor and got on antidepressants. I called my youngest sister to tell her I couldn't make it to her college graduation. (Any woman in our family graduating from college is a big deal.) I emailed the board of the nonprofit and told them I was taking the month off. I deleted social media apps from my phone.

I knew I was going to make it. But I didn't *know* I was going to make it. It was one of the worst episodes of depression I've experienced to date.

I have spent decades carving out the life I want, going against deeply ingrained cultural and familial beliefs. Part of my journey is shedding the belief that if I do all the right things, my life will be amazing, free of pain and trials.

That isn't reality. It's a false promise straight from religiosity. In creating a different ending—a better ending—for myself, I am releasing myself from the expectation that my life will be without difficulty. Part of this better ending is learning to hold the sad and scary things alongside all the truly beautiful and happy things. Neither define my life or consume my identity.

My life will never be pain-free. But that doesn't mean my life will be void of laughter or celebration.

The behavior of the volunteer that sent me into a months-long season of depression stepped on several of my insecurities and fears.

But she also exposed these fears for what they were: crippling and confining. I battled voices that told me I couldn't be a leader. Those voices taunted me when I failed by letting an unhealthy person work with the nonprofit, parading my failure in front of me as evidence I never should have thought I could do this in the first place.

I had to learn to stare those voices down and admit I'd made mistakes, but mistakes are not disqualification. Many expect perfection from leaders who are women. I fight this culture by not expecting perfection from myself, only growth.

Telling a volunteer who sucked life from the organization that she needed to step down makes me the sort of leader who is willing to face consequences for their choices. It makes me the sort of leader I'd want to work with. It makes me someone with preferences who is willing to put those preferences out in the universe, expecting results.

It also makes me the sort of leader many won't want to work with. I have to accept that I won't be liked by everyone.

I also had to acknowledge I feared becoming a narcissist. But this fear was based in ignorance about the characteristics of narcissists. Narcissists are fragmented individuals. They are fragmented from a sense of self and live in an alternate reality—one where some parameters of human dignity do not apply to them. My connection to myself, my awareness of my limitations and fears, are the very things that signify I am becoming more integrated with myself.

A couple weeks after going on meds, I flew out to the West Coast for a meeting with the company I worked for. I'm not sure I could have physically made the trip without the antidepressants.

A few days before the trip, a small glimmer of excitement pierced a hole in the menacing cloud that shrouded my life. I clung to that glimmer. It foretold the storm would not last forever.

I arrived a couple days early so I could see old friends. My friend Carol and I went to dinner and a show. I met up with folks at the only ramen place I like in the entire world. I stayed with my friend Samantha, the one I went to Scotland with. Two friends met up with me on different days to cowork over coffee. I had dinner with friends at one of my favorite speakeasies.

The trip was laughter, friendship, and sunshine. (Nothing beats the Pacific Coast sun.) The meds might have been kicking in by then, but the trip gave me a reset. Part of it was being in a place I loved. The other part was being around people I like who like me back.

I don't know about you, but one of the main voices in my head during depression is the voice that says nobody likes me and everyone thinks I'm too much to handle. There aren't many feelings worse than knowing the main thing you need to help navigate depression is the friendship of others, but your inner voices are telling you everyone hates you, so you avoid the very people you need.

I haven't come up with a solution to this dichotomy, but friends who've pushed past these voices—even when they didn't know they were doing it—are the ones who've helped me each time one of these episodes occurs. During this trauma season, Martha knew I was going through a rough time, so she met me for coffee and brought me a bouquet of flowers. I started crying right there in the coffee shop. Those tears were a release and a doorway to receiving love.

It's nice to have other friends who experience depression and who will talk about what it's like. Those are the best ones to go to, because they're the least likely to shame you or hint that you should just try harder to get it together. Folks who pressure you to try harder are the worst type of people for those with depression, because nobody puts more pressure on a depressed person than the depressed person themselves.

My colleague Laura Anderson says that we can't "unlearn" things. Once messages have an opportunity to create neural pathways in the plasticity of our brains, they stay there. However, we can create new neural pathways that are stronger than the old ones.

My depression told me I was unlikeable and that I deserved all the bad things that were happening to me. Then I flew to the West Coast, placing my body in a different environment. I spent time with friends who were excited to see me, hourly countering the message that nobody liked me. The trip didn't make the messages from my depression go away. But the new messages became louder, brighter, stronger.

The messages from our traumaversaries may never disappear, but we have opportunities to create new messages, new memories, new anniversaries. We can take back our lives and our stories, one small, bright spot of joy at a time.

FIFTEEN: RELIGION

How We Made It

RITUAL

In the support groups for Tears of Eden, one topic we address with spiritual abuse survivors is the rituals of spiritual practice. For those of us who now experience pain around things like worship music, prayer and scripture, we often grieve the loss of religious tradition. For example, there's something beautiful and mystical in gathering with others to take communion. We say the words, eat the bread, drink from the cup. It can be familiar and comfortable—even if we don't always understand what it means.

But when we experience abuse that causes trauma in the context of this spiritual community, anything associated with that community can activate panic, emotional pain, flashbacks, or other trauma responses. Some push through the pain in order to be "good Christians." Some flee the pain altogether, taking an indefinite break.

Some discover, during the break, that they no longer believe.

Wherever someone may land on this spectrum, wherever someone might be on the journey, we encourage survivors to notice the human attraction to ritual and tradition. It connects us to others in the present day. It also connects us to our ancestors, to the ages of tradition that came before.

We lose so much when we lose our spiritual community. We don't just lose church on Sunday, we lose connection to an entire history. It's a loss as deep as losing a hundred loved ones. In a sense, that's exactly what we've lost.

Like with any loss or grief, there is a period of mourning. After the loss of a loved one, everyone says the first year is the hardest. You go through each phase of your life and notice for the first time in each phase that the person is no longer with you. You are reminded anew of this loss during each yearly mile marker. You really can't skip this part. You can try to hold the tears in, but they'll just show up in another form. Let yourself cry. Let yourself wail if you need to. Rage at the heavens. Break something that won't cause any permanent damage. I like to break ice cubes on the pavement—the sound of cracking when the ice hits asphalt is a cathartic release.

Once you've gone through that first year, you might be in a place where you can create new traditions. Maybe you incorporate some of the old ones, because the memories are still tender and you don't want to forget.

Maybe you make something completely new. Maybe instead of a pot roast at Christmas, you make a lasagna instead. Instead of church on Sunday, maybe you meet friends for brunch. Instead of reading the Bible in the morning, maybe you read one of Emily Dickinson's poems. Instead of prayer, maybe you meditate, sitting on a pillow on the floor, encircled by your favorite crystals.

Whatever you decide to do, don't skip the grief. It may rise up unexpectedly for years to come. Welcome those tears. Befriend your anger. Write curses for the people who hurt you on pieces of paper—then burn the pieces.

This loss is worthy of your grief. You deserve an opportunity to mourn.

WITCHES

Christmas Eve. My friend Heather and I spent the day on an adorable historical street lined with brick buildings and cottages vending local wares. Actors dressed in Victorian garb walked the cobblestones and sang carols for patrons.

We stopped in a crystal shop, a place Heather had once met a real witch. I bought two crystals for mental clarity and decision-making. Heather introduced me to palo santo, a plant that is burned like incense to relieve stress and pain and to remove negative energy. I bought a stick to take home—hoping to cleanse my apartment of the trauma and stress it seemed to hold, impacting my sleep.

We spent the rest of the evening watching thriller movies. (We both enjoy them. We just prefer to watch them with a friend.) After a dinner of pot roast and gluten-free cheese biscuits, I asked Heather to show me how to use the palo santo. She lit the end of the stick and waved the essence over me, encouraging the spirits to release what no longer served.

Then she brought out her witch kit: a tray hidden beneath her TV stand. She made us tea and lit incense. I shuffled her deck of oracle cards and placed them on my chest. I felt prompted to draw five cards from the middle of the deck. The cards seemed to follow a theme of staying true to myself and the path I had chosen, which corresponded with what I'd already been feeling during that season: that I had everything I needed to make the decision that was best for me.

As we sat talking about the future and sipping our tea, I saw flashes of aura zipping Tinker-Bell-like about the space. I told Heather, and she welcomed the spirit and anything it wanted to say. I got the sense it was friendly, bringing an energy of playfulness.

The reality that Heather and I both hold seminary degrees from a Christian institution and had once had robust careers in ministry felt perfectly in sync with where we found ourselves. Rather than a contradiction, our religious education complemented our comfort with a connection to a world beyond what we could see. For all Christianity's seeming aversion to magic and witches, the religion calls its followers to believe the fantastical. Take Christmas, for example. God was born in human form to an unwed mother who'd never had intercourse. Angels appeared to shepherds. The stars guided pagan kings to find a child.

Even the practice of ritual, of connecting to the spiritual, we learned from Christianity.

We learned harmful things from Christianity, too. Like an addiction to certainty and a mistrust of the feminine. For several years, I had to take a break from it all. Pain and trauma overwhelmed this religion I loved. I could no longer stomach the prayers and the songs and the verses.

But as Heather and I interacted with the oracle cards, it held a kinship with prayer. I remembered what it was once like to pray with my friends—to beseech the heavens for our desires. Once we believed in an all-powerful God. Yet when you send up prayers to the all-powerful and those prayers go unanswered, it can lead to grief and confusion. Conversely, interacting with the divine of the earth and the divine within felt less certain but somehow more creative and peaceful to us. It felt freer. I felt an active participant in my own life and my future, instead of simply waiting for things beyond my control to happen to me.

Some expressions of Christianity encourage communion and partnership with the Creator. This Creator created us to live and create alongside them. The Creator is benevolent and allows their creation to choose good in the world. This Creator gave their creation desires and grieves when the creation denies those desires out of a misplaced belief that denial is holy.

ADOPTION

My sister Macey and her husband pursued adoption after the birth of their first child. I can't begin to understand the consternation of the waiting, the hope that a mother would choose them, only to have those hopes dashed when the mother changed her mind or went with another family. Over and over, they went through the process. Three years of riding the roller coaster of excitement, grief, waiting, hope, and disappointment.

Macey would post regular updates on Facebook about the adoption process. She'd sandwich her expression of grief with some message about the goodness of God, proclaiming her commitment to trust that God had a good plan in process—a plan she and her husband couldn't see or grasp.

I'll admit I sometimes rolled my eyes when I read these messages. *Just express your grief! You don't have to qualify it with some arbitrary praise or forced gratitude.* Sometimes I'd just skip the posts and wouldn't read them. The preaching irked me as I grieved for my sister's circumstances in my own way. I may not know what it's like to wait to adopt a child, but I know what it's like to wait and have hopes continually disappointed. I wanted to support her, but I just couldn't stomach all the gospel shit I'd have to wade through to get to her side.

Then one day, it hit me. As another "God is good" post floated past my feed, I realized: This *was* my sister's grief. This was how she processed. This was how she sought comfort. She sought out a deity she believed was good. She mystically placed her sadness and pain in this deity's hands. She used the energy of her grief to express gratitude because it brought her moments of peace. It helped her make sense of something that seems senseless. It helped her feel less out of control. It helped her smile and care for the child she already had. It helped her get out of bed and go to work and go about her daily life.

Praising God was how she coped. It's possible some part of this was the denial stage of her grief—a very human phase so many of us go through. But who am I to deny someone the practice and ritual that helps them navigate their trauma?

While I believe at some point we have to face grief head-on, we have to feel those emotions in our blood and bones, and we have to let that cycle complete, I also believe we are not always ready to do that. And each individual gets to decide when that time is right for them.

If Jesus helps someone get through an excruciating season, then Jesus is their answer.

VIKINGS

After I left the chronically abusive West Coast church, Christianity and anything to do with Christianity used to cause a lot of pain. If someone started praying, I'd run from the room. If I was at a conference and they started playing praise music, I'd hide in the bathroom. My dear friends would send me their sermons to listen to or read, and I'd do the best I could, skipping over the sections of scripture so I could give encouragement or feedback. This was especially disheartening when I remembered how much I used to love the Bible—so much so that I went to school for a master's just so I could study it more.

Then one day, I crossed over the hump. I went from one side to the other. I went from cringing and caving in on myself to having a calm and indifferent perspective. I no longer threw up or got clammy when someone started talking about how much they loved Jesus. The *Vikings* show on the History Channel helped carry me on my passage toward this new equilibrium. Art and story typically play a role in most of my major seasons of life. This time was incredibly obvious.

In the show, Ragnar, a Viking, captures Athelstan, a Christian monk. Over the years, they move from captive-and-master to partners and friends. Athelstan becomes Ragnar's advisor, and Ragnar teaches his people to have respect for the Christian and his beliefs. Ragnar and Athelstan argue about who is the true God: Odin or the god of the Christians. The Vikings believed Odin hung on a tree for nine days. This story is not unlike the story of Jesus hanging on a tree and rising from the dead in three days. The two men argue and debate and have lively conversations.

During one episode, Ragnar and Athelstan share a moment in which they both admit that in worshiping Odin and in worshiping the god of the Christians, they might be worshiping the same god.

And that's when it changed for me. Ragnar and Athelstan had no idea I was following their journey with interest, curious how it would end. Despite the pain Christianity had caused me, I rationally could not find a reason to burn it all to the ground and declare religion a farce.

Then there it was, in the journey of two men on opposite sides of the religious spectrum, slowly moving toward one another to arrive at the center—to one thing they might have in common.

Really, it started before that, with their common humanity and respect for one another. They tiptoed nearer and nearer with every debate. Their arguments became rooted in their friendship and mutual respect rather than in being right.

I believe I chose my master's degree in religion and cultures with genuine excitement, out of an interest in studying humanity. Both religion and culture are intricately interwoven with one another, shaping each other. Both are shaped by humanity. Both, in turn, shape humanity.

Religion is part of what it means to be human. We all look for something to explain the unexplainable, like why evil exists or what happens after we die. We look for comfort and security during times of great sorrow, like when we lose a loved one or when we find out we have terminal cancer. We know there are things beyond. Forces we cannot see. We feel threads of life swirling about us. Sometimes we feel like *someone* is directing from the great beyond.

Religions form out of seeking the unknown, attempting to explain what cannot be explained. Some people call it science. Some call it faith. Each individual chooses what they will trust, what they will believe.

Sometimes someone comes along and says they have all the answers. Because most people struggle and live within states of confusion, they'll gravitate toward the priest or pastor or guru who offers assurance and certainty. Within this dynamic, sometimes their freedom to believe is taken away. Sometimes, before they know it, their agency and autonomy have been removed.

This part of religion is what leads to the sort of abuse I experienced, when someone commandeers it for their own gain. It's no different than someone forcing sex upon you. Indeed, sexual abuse and spiritual abuse are known to cause similar damage. Some survivors of both say the spiritual abuse is worse.

It's understandable that when religion has been a weapon used to cause harm, we learn to hate that weapon. Fear it. Flee it. We rage against it and warn others to stay away. One of the harmful things religion taught me was that I could only be friends with people who believed what I believed. This is a toxic teaching that leads to elitism, classism, and a whole lot of other isms that cause damage and leave people traumatized.

One of the things I'm learning on the other side of an abusive expression of religion is that I can hold space for people who think differently than I do. I can learn and grow with others who are on different paths. So if someone lands on the path of no religion after religious abuse, I get it. I thought I might follow that path myself; I still might.

As it is, I can't fault the ritual of religion. Religion is a source of our collective humanity. Most religions have some core beliefs that resemble each other. Many world religions have more in common than they have differences, though I'm sure a lot of orthodox believers will resent me for saying this. Religions thrive on being different and offering something the rest of the world cannot offer. It's the main tenet of their marketing campaign.

Yet the bare bones of religion is the heart cry of people who are searching for comfort, for a way to explain the unexplainable. Our world is often cold, harsh, and callous. I won't begrudge someone who finds comfort and meaning in a religious practice, in trusting in a higher power.

SIXTEEN: CREATIVITY

Inventing the Life We Want

CRAWLING BACKWARD

The story was part of our family folklore, told anew to each house-guest or dinner guest. By the time I was a young adolescent, I'd heard it so many times that I could tell it verbatim, though I had no memory of it. The event occurred when I was not yet old enough to walk but old enough to understand my mother's call.

She was in her room, calling me to come to her, but when I did not respond after she said my name several times, she assumed I was ignoring her to get into some mischief.

When she poked her head out of her bedroom door and into the hallway, what she discovered was not an errant child but a perfectly obedient one, dutifully responding toward her mother's beckoning. Yet that child wasn't crawling toward her in a forward-thrusting trajectory. She was crawling backward.

At first glance, you might have thought the child was confused about the mechanics of crawling, yet the baby crawled backward with all the confidence of an explorer discovering new territory.

I may not remember the incident, but I can imagine how my infant brain came up with this scheme. Indeed, it's the way I often come up with schemes in the present day. I can imagine I heard my mother's call and, as usual, responded by heading in her direction.

Then a thought popped into my mind: *Why do we crawl forward? Is it because it's the way it's always been done? Has anyone ever tried to do it differently? Maybe there's another way to crawl. Maybe it isn't faster, but perhaps it is more fun. I'll go backward and see what it's like. Ah! This is interesting. Wait until Mommy sees this. She's going to get a real kick out of my ingenuity. She might start telling her friends I'm a baby genius. Look at me now!*

Crawling backward isn't faster, and it isn't more efficient. My mother did not think I was a genius. She thought I was strange. And entertaining. As far as I know, I never tried it again. But my creativity earned me the nickname Weird Bird from my parents. The name stuck for over a decade and still surfaced from time to time in my teen years and early adulthood.

I'm convinced one reason I got out of a cult in my mid-twenties, and later an abusive church system in my mid-thirties, is because of my approach to life that led me to experiment with crawling backward down the hallway. I have an innate propensity to question the status quo. I also do not fit into systems that expect everyone to behave a certain way, undervaluing individuality and suppressing independent thought. Because I do not fit, those systems become progressively uncomfortable and confining. They eventually become so suffocating that I have to make a choice between shriveling up and dying on the inside or taking a risk that things will be better if I leave.

Most mainstream stories about surviving cults tend to conclude shortly after the person escapes. Society at large is drawn to the drama and sensationalism of what happens inside. But most of the true journey to freedom happens during the after years. There's a saying among cult survivors: "You can leave the cult, but the cult doesn't always leave you." Writing new messages after the old ones are ingrained in our bodies takes years of work, struggle, and grief. And it's difficult to rewrite those messages if you stumble into a world that resembles the cult you escaped—even if that world is just different enough to make you feel like you're finally safe. What kept us inside the cult will often lead us to seek out another similar system for the sake of familiarity.

But here's another idea. What if the same resources that helped us escape, even the rejection we experience, will continue to help us grow and heal on the other side?

I've always questioned things—even if most of those questions stayed in my head because it wasn't safe to utter them aloud. My life has been plagued by an incessant need to try new things, to experiment. In every job I've ever had, I've come up with an idea that makes most folks balk. It takes some hand-holding (and tactful cajoling) to see my ideas through. Most of the time, my vision enhances the vision of the organization—taking things to the next level. I'm a next-leveler. A visionary. An inventor.

This sort of person will not survive inside of a high-control environment. This sort of person will suffocate under surveillance. They'll eventually have a meltdown under micromanagement. When I was trapped inside the system, this led to a lot of deceit. I learned how to leave out information that might get me in trouble. I learned to hide, to keep secrets, to fly under the radar.

But these survival mechanisms are not sustainable. Hiding became unbearable. The biggest secret I ever kept was my plot to escape.

Who I am saved my life. Choosing myself and tapping into the resources I had got me out. I was the wrong sort of person for the system. The antibodies of the system attacked the foreign substance (me) and made the environment so uncomfortable the substance dispelled itself.

It can be incredibly painful (often traumatizing) to constantly feel like you're out of place. At the same time, my out-of-placeness was my superpower. I hear stories like mine all the time. A small child raises their hand to verify the Bible logic of their Sunday school teacher, only to be shamed and shut down for daring to seek clarification. While they may learn to stop asking questions, they never forget the sting. That sting lingers and lingers until eventually the child grows up and decides they will no longer be silent.

It hurts to be rejected. That pain is absolutely real. But how often do we acknowledge that rejection as a gift? The X-wing cruiser that carried us away from the *Death Star*?

Here is an exercise I invite my clients to engage in: Take a moment to write down all the things about you the system said were bad.

Then flip that list around and write out how each of those things helped you recognize something was wrong with the system. How did they help you wake up? How did they help you get to freedom?

Of course the system didn't like those things about you. It rightfully saw those things for what they were: dangerous to its control.

MISTAKES

After a year working in Mexico, I moved to the Midwest to attend seminary. While there, I joined a poetry club. The only poem I ever read to the group was a poem called "The Rules." I only remember a few lines from it, but in essence, it was a poem about the rules for me growing up. Things like, "Your father is always right. Even if he is wrong, he is right. But make sure you tell him if he's making a mistake; if you don't, the mistake is your fault." Another line said, "Make sure you homeschool your kids. If you don't, you doom America."

I sent the poem to my siblings. My sisters all responded to say they cried when they read it. My brothers did not respond, but I heard through the sibling gossip chain that they disagreed with the poem. I heard they said, "That's not the way it was."

My siblings and I received different messages based on our gender. My brothers were raised to be kings of their households one day. My sisters and I were raised to always be a support system to a man.

Just this one difference had a huge impact on our approaches to life. My brothers walk into a space and believe they deserve to be there, whether they have earned the right or not. Of course they deserved the job, the promotion, the raise, the credit. My sisters and I fight against our tendency to hold ourselves back. We show up in a space prepared to spend a good long time proving we belong there. Each one of us navigates imposter syndrome. We all have stories of turning down presented opportunities because we didn't feel qualified.

I'll speak for myself when I say very little of this is conscious. Most of the time I don't realize I'm self-sabotaging until I've already sabotaged. These messages are embedded into my bones, creeping up into crippling fear whenever I'm trying something new, whenever I'm leading, whenever the responsibility is on me.

These things are scary for anyone, but if you were told most of your life that it was wrong for you to lead, to expect, to express, then forthrightness and directness will often feel like you're betraying yourself—even when it's the opposite.

Perhaps you've heard this saying: "We teach our girls to be perfect but we teach our boys to be brave." These two different teachings produce different outcomes. One gender is taught to not make a mistake. One gender is taught to be bold, with an implication that mistakes are a part of the process. Or perhaps they don't consider mistakes to be mistakes at all.

Our society is not a safe place for women to try things, fail, and try again. Even though I left a cult that prohibited me from so many things because I was a woman, I entered the world, and it was still unkind to women.

How are we supposed to heal when there are so many messages in the wider world that resemble the messages we received in high-control religion?

How are sects like the one my family was a part of ever going to disappear when there are so many messages in the wider world corroborating my father's beliefs?

When I moved back to the Midwest in 2021, I started taking improv classes. My motivation was a desire to be better at thinking on my feet, not getting caught off guard when something I scripted got interrupted. I had no intention of performing. In fact, I'd never seen an improv performance before I started taking classes. Call it a compulsion, but I often feel the need to take everything I do to the next level. I have had to strong-arm myself to not turn yoga into something monetary and keep it a practice I do just for myself. Every day, I'm in danger of getting a certification and starting to teach classes. But so far, I've guarded this practice, saving it for my self-care alone.

With improv, level one became level two and level two became level three. Before I knew it, I was on stage and performing with a team: making mistakes, laughing our asses off, spawning ridiculous scenarios in the span of a few moments.

Improv is high-level performance art, but people often don't take it seriously because it is comedy. It's the AV club of the theater world and is often the butt of jokes in shows and movies. While I can delude myself into thinking I can perfect the art of writing (sometimes believing I've already perfected it), no one can perfect improv. You are literally making up scenes and storylines in real time. With a team. While an audience watches.

No one will ever be perfect at improv. All we will ever do is grow. In fact, "mistakes" are often great comedic moments and opportunities for your scene partners to turn your mistakes into source material for the next scene.

But mistakes have always carried more weight for me. The first time friends outside of improv came to watch one of my shows, I didn't have a good night. I was exhausted and stressed from work. I'd missed practice the week before. A number of factors contributed to me making some basic blunders. I could perform so much better, but my friends didn't know that. They didn't know very much about improv, either, and probably didn't know I'd messed up.

However, that night I experienced a fierce shame spiral. The words *I hate myself* played on a loop in my brain. The intensity of the shame spiral lasted all night, preventing me from getting sleep. While the intensity lessened throughout the next few days, I was still in a spiral when I got to therapy the next week. I knew the shame was out of proportion with what happened, but knowing the truth and communicating that truth to your body are separate paths, and one often takes longer than the other.

The first thing I had to do was separate the shame from the critique. My performance wasn't great. That was truth. I had room to grow and improve. That was truth also.

Then I had to assess the shame. Where did the glaring sense of *I hate myself* come from? Well, this was rooted in what I mentioned in the poem "The Rules." It wasn't safe to fail in my family of origin. In fact, it was genuinely dangerous to make mistakes. I could never just let a mistake be, laugh it off, and move on. I had to pay for them, sometimes in extremely humiliating and painful ways.

Then I started my vocation in ministry—working on staff in churches. I wanted to be a teacher in a world where that job normally fell to men. I'd fight for those opportunities, but because I didn't have much practice at teaching, I was, naturally, not that great in the beginning.

Even with limited experience, I felt the pressure to be excellent. I wasn't just representing myself, I was representing all womankind. When I'd blunder a speaking or teaching opportunity, no one was there to talk me through it, help me understand the experience, and tell me to get back out there and try again. If I foiled an opportunity simply out of inexperience, my performance directly impacted opportunities I received in the future, in that I would not receive them again.

Men who were teachers were given ample opportunities to try and fail and try again. Women received few opportunities. When they did get those opportunities, they were expected to excel, even though they didn't have as much experience as their male counterparts. In my vocation, failure wasn't an option. Just like it wasn't an option in my family. If I made mistakes, I suffered.

So when I look at that shame spiral I experienced after my improv performance, I know where it comes from. It comes from an outside source, and those people and systems are to blame. I know it's not my fault. I'm allowed to make mistakes. I'm allowed to grow. I'm allowed to fail and get back up and try again.

The fact that there is no certain point in the future where I will ever be perfect at improv is simultaneously frustrating and freeing. I am forced to settle into the moment, enjoy the journey from two-line scenes to more complex collisions of worlds, time, and themes. I am learning to present my mistakes to the team and audience with a posture of "I meant to do that," saying yes to myself as much as I say yes to others.

I'm learning how to laugh at mistakes. I'm learning how to have fun without barriers. I never really knew how to have fun before.

THE GIFT

I'm in a dusky green meadow
With waving, bending grass
A little girl approaches
A girl I know so well
Standing there in front of me
Her face reflects my own

In her hands, she holds a box
Wrapped with string and bow
All at once I'm crying
Speaking to the girl:

I'm sorry that they hurt you
For the fearful life you had
I'm sorry you were happy
But beneath it all was sad.

I wish I could have saved you
And told you how to fight
I wish I could have held you
While you shed tears on your bed at night

The little girl takes my hand
Eyes a shiny blue
"Inside this box,
I have a gift for you."

I take the box
Unwrap it slow
My hands a trembling mess
What memory will the box reveal?
I lift the lid with dread

I gasp a bit
Surprised delight
I smile at the girl
She smiles back
And hops away, calling,
"Say what you want to say."

My heart skips two beats
Before it speaks
The gift is strong and clear
I accept the gift
A deliberate choice
And turn it all around
I use my words
And thank the girl
For she's gifted my own voice

FICTION

My debut novel, *Hartfords*, released when I was thirty-six years old. I made sure my mother knew I did not want my father at the book signing in my hometown. A few years before this, I had finally and completely severed my relationship with my father. The only reason I'd held on to the relationship at all had to do with a damaging Christian teaching that we must always leave room for the offender to repent, which is just another way of saying the offense never happened.

Grief is a strange emotion. It has no timeline. Often it doesn't follow logic. Waves will hit you out of nowhere. A tsunami hit me one morning years after my father was no longer a part of my life.

It happened while I was writing. Fiction has a way of getting at the truth deep in our core.

The scene I was writing was a conversation between a father and daughter. The daughter is trying to decide if she wants to marry her boyfriend. The father is listening and assuring his daughter that he trusts her to make the right choice and that he will support her whatever decision she makes.

The wave gave no warning before the mass of it hit me in the chest and consumed my whole body. I began weeping. Tears like a waterfall began running down my face.

I would never have a father like the character in my story.

I would never have a father who would support me no matter what choice I made.

I would never have a father who would trust me to make good decisions.

I would never have a father who would keep copies of my book in his house just so he could show them off to his friends: "Look, look, my daughter wrote a book."

I would never have a father who was capable of being proud of his daughter.

I would never have a father who was capable of loving me the way I needed.

The tears continued to flow off and on throughout the day. The mass of grief continued to press against my chest for days.

I felt the strangeness of grieving the loss of a person I never had in the first place. Fictionalizing a tender relationship between a father and a daughter—I knew what that relationship looked like, but I had never, and would never, experience that sort of tenderness from a parent in real life. Every moment of perceived tenderness with my father paraded before me in its true colors: My father only mimicked love. I don't believe he ever actually felt it.

I understand why people want to hang on to shards and shreds of a relationship with an abusive parent. It is excruciating to acknowledge the hole left by an absent, cruel parent.

The absence of a loving, supportive father is worthy of all my grief. I don't expect my grief for such a loss will ever fully end. I don't expect the challenge of navigating the waters of my future career and relationships without the support of my parents will ever disappear completely.

I can continue to create tender moments between fathers and daughters in books. Fiction sometimes reveals the deepest longings of our hearts—creating avenues to grieve the dreams we've lost. The dreams we didn't know we had.

It is for this reason I prioritize the creative in my life. It is for this reason I encourage my clients and friends to explore their creative sides. Art allows us to access our intuition—that little voice inside of us that reflects our true selves.

Abusive environments chip away at our true selves. They whittle us down to hollow versions that obey (or obsessively keep trying to). They twist the gifts we might offer freely for the good of the collective by commandeering those gifts—demanding them—coercing them from us so we do not remember those gifts belong to us. These abusive environments will name certain gifts dangerous. The ones they cannot control, they will seek to eradicate altogether.

Creating, breathing life into ourselves, is one way we give ourselves the compassion and tenderness we always deserved—the sort our abusers were incapable of giving, the sort that was starved and beaten out of us.

When we write, paint, sing, dance, perform, or bake purely for our own enjoyment, when we give ourselves over to the sensations of the present moment, that little version of us the abusers crushed and shoved into a corner removes its little hands from covering its fearful eyes. *Someone wants to see me?* it whispers. *Someone cares about how I feel? About what I want to say?*

Yes, we say back. Gently, we coax our true selves out from hiding. We clear away the rubble from the catastrophic destruction caused by a hostile regime. We make mosaics out of the rubble. We write songs out of the destruction.

We create the lives we were always meant to live.

SEVENTEEN: LAUGHTER

I Believe You

REALITY

"PTSD: the gift that keeps on giving," I texted to my sister Elizabeth, reacting to the ongoing, seemingly inexplicable health struggles I was having. I was working with multiple doctors, most of whom told me I was fine. "Just exercise and maybe try to lose ten pounds." This medical admonition landed on my frustrated ears as one of my health struggles was that I *was* working out consistently and eating healthy. Yet not only was I unable to lose weight, somehow I kept gaining it.

Seriously?

Doctors didn't seem concerned, but when blood work revealed high cortisol levels, which seemed to explain my ongoing sleep issues, I kept looking and digging.

My study of trauma taught me to listen to my body. My body was telling me something wasn't right, and my intuition hypothesized that the culprit was a lifetime of chronic stress.

After I left an abusive, high-control environment in my mid-twenties, I spent the next decade navigating financial struggles, career struggles, toxic bosses and workplaces, and ongoing interactions with abusive and toxic family members.

Health challenges and two bad bouts of depression that had a significant physical impact on my body caused me to start overhauling my life and eliminating present-day stressors. But this overhauling wasn't enough to address the decades of trauma still clinging to my nervous system.

Spiritual abuse affects everything. Understandably, it causes existential and spiritual impact. But we don't always talk about the other areas of our lives that experience destruction. Spiritual abuse takes a sledgehammer to nearly every domain. We experience impact on our physical bodies, community and social circles, relationships, careers, and finances. Those of us who had to move to get away from abusive communities or workplaces have experienced geographic impacts.

It causes monumental damage.

We will never be the same.

The thousand tiny paper cuts of this insidious form of abuse may start to heal, but the scars—they are permanent.

This may be reality, but there's another reality: Thriving after abuse isn't contingent on being fully healed.

We can live thriving, full lives, even while our bodies are *healing*.

I suspect the impact of what I experienced means I will be healing for the rest of my life. I don't imagine there will ever be a day that I stop going to therapy or a day when I won't have to make some concessions in my life because of post-traumatic stress or complex trauma.

For example, I have decided not to have children because the stress of birthing and raising a child is not something I want to put my body through, no matter how wonderful the experience of having kids might be.

However, with this choice, I'm giving myself other wonderful options. I have more financial options, more time for myself and my creative projects, opportunities to travel, emotional space and capacity to invest in friends and my chosen family, and a lot less stress.

I can live a vibrant, thriving life, even in the aftermath of abuse.

Today, I'm still addressing some of the health issues I've been having, working with trauma-informed specialists, hoping to give my body what it needs to keep healing itself. I think I'm making progress, but sometimes I wonder if I'm living in the new normal.

Thriving doesn't mean all is well all the time, which isn't reality for anyone. When our lives have been indefinitely altered by the trauma from abuse, we might experience the fallout every single day.

And…

We can learn to hold this reality alongside the reality that this impact does not mean we've lost the opportunity to heal and thrive.

We are whole, even with the scars.

I acknowledge that, for some, thriving is a distant flash of lightning on the horizon, something far away that we're uncertain may ever come. A good day is one where we manage to make it out of bed and eat a somewhat-normal meal.

That's okay. At least half of my clients have heard me say, "The fastest way to healing is slow." Even as I say this, I wish it weren't so. I wish there were a pill or a surgery or a four-day retreat that would speed that healing along—just a little bit faster. (Maybe the field of neuroscience will invent something someday.)

Our wise bodies heal when they heal. We aid our healing when we give our body what it needs, listening and trusting it after high-control religion told us we could not trust ourselves.

Two focuses that aid the healing process on the other side of spiritual abuse are validation and finding and creating the language to name what happened to us. The naming is so important in spiritual abuse because of the subtleness, the confusing nature, the invisibleness of the cuts. Having language to name the experience is a form of validation. "Oh, there's a term for *that*? It's an actual *thing*?"

To further this validation is the experience of encountering others who have been there. Who believe us. Who can tell us what happened to us mattered, and mattered, and mattered. It's not a blip on the timeline of history we can erase. It's important. It's real.

We deserve the opportunity to meet others who know.

LAUGHTER

I hadn't met anyone outside of my family who had grown up the way I had and was willing to talk about it. I didn't know anyone else who could name my experience as abuse and understand the deep impact Christian patriarchy had on every aspect of my life. Almost no one recognized it as a cult.

Then I met Cait.

Cait and I connected through Instagram. We had both grown up in the stay-at-home-daughter movement (I learned this phrase for my upbringing from Cait) and had started publicly sharing our experiences. We were both writers. After two years of interacting over social media, we finally got to meet in person for the first time.

Several social media advocates united in Chicago for a conference. Most of us had never met in person; we'd only interacted online. The first night, we migrated toward one another in the hotel restaurant. After several drinks, we were laughing over the main thing that had brought us to the conference: abuse in the church.

We were laughing.

About abuse.

It was cathartic. My chest swelled with relief to be in the company of a dozen people who understood and were willing to talk about it.

The following night, we were out at dinner again. It was the last night, so we lingered and lingered and eventually took the party back to the hotel bar. Cait and I were sitting next to one another, and a mutual friend, whose spiritual abuse story was different than ours, asked us how we met.

There comes a time in life where just the right question unlocks a longing you did not know you had. You may never have known you wanted someone to ask, or known you desired an opportunity to share, about the very thing requested of you. Then the rush of relief uncovers this buried gem of your story, hidden deep in the cave of subconscious.

To answer this question, Cait and I introduced the similarities of our families of origin. We volleyed back and forth, telling stories of our upbringings that were so eerily similar, we momentarily played with the idea that we might have the same father. We considered if we might be long-lost sisters and our father had a secret family.

Then we remembered this delightful tool known as the internet and looked up photos of our fathers, confirming we were not love children. Oh well, it was nice to ponder the possibility.

With each laughter-encased story, we witnessed the eyes of our friend who had asked the question get wider and wider. After somewhere around forty-five minutes, this friend asked, "Do you hate your dads?"

"I don't," I answered. "I feel like I have reached a place where I have deep compassion for the pain he's causing himself."

Cait echoed that she didn't hate her father, either.

Our friend asked, "Is it okay if I hate your dads for you?"

"Go right ahead," I said. "I think my father is a terrible person."

Since that first in-person connection, Cait and I have had the opportunity to be together a half-dozen more times. Currently, we're both editors and writers for Tears of Eden. I bought several copies of Cait's memoir, *Rift*, for friends and family who had grown up the way we had. Until *Rift*, the only other memoir I'd read that captured what I'd experienced growing up was *Educated* by Tara Westover.

Validation. Relief. Release. That's what it feels like to meet someone (in person or in writing) who went through something similar and can name it for what it actually is.

Lots of people have been abused in their families and in the church. Often they've inherited the toxic positivity of their culture and believe they've experienced healing from the Lord as long as they can smile and claim they have radically forgiven their abuser. But smiling faces sometimes mask the trauma festering in our marrow—secretly spreading and building pressure the longer it goes unaddressed. One thing that helps us release this pressure and engage with our trauma is when we share the story over a cup of coffee with someone who can say, "I believe you, because I've been there, too."

CAMARADERIE

At 11 p.m. on a Saturday, I arrived back at my apartment from a day at the in-person retreat Tears of Eden hosted in my city. Heart full after a day spent with other spiritual abuse survivors and stomach full of the Italian sub I'd just finished at the pub down the street from my place, I was just closing my door and kicking off my shoes when a filmmaker named Lucy texted: "Are you awake?"

"Just got home. Wide awake!"

"Can I give a quick call? Faster than texting."

Instead of replying, I selected the phone symbol.

She answered "We haven't had that much time to talk to just you. Would it be okay if we filmed you in the morning?"

"Sure. Like when?"

"What time do events start tomorrow?"

"Breakfast is at 9 a.m."

"Okay. Could we come to you at 7?"

"Wait…like, come here?"

"Yeah, we'd want to film you getting ready. Getting dressed. Putting on makeup."

"Oh you're going to be in my apartment?" I frantically looked around at my space, recognizing the impact of a week of prepping for the Tears of Eden event. Four used coffee cups looked like they were holding a support group on my kitchen table. My clean laundry hung across the back of my bed. Clothes. Shoes. Papers. Trash. Unclean dishes. "Er, my apartment is a mess right now."

"That's okay. We want it to be natural, and we don't want to cause any extra stress. Don't worry about cleaning anything."

I thought, *Yeah, right,* but agreed they could come film.

Lucy said, "See you in the morning. Get some sleep."

I hung up and immediately started throwing dirty dishes in my dishwasher. I was still pretty energized from the day and told myself I'd sleep better if my apartment was clean.

I managed to be in bed just after midnight, not expecting to sleep much. I hadn't slept much the night before either. What the hell. I just had a documentary film crew coming to my house at 7 a.m. No big deal. They said they wanted natural. Natural was what they were going to get.

I ended up falling asleep immediately and waking up at 6 a.m. to my alarm clock. I jetted out of bed and put on clothes because I *would* be wearing a bra before I was in front of a camera.

The documentary crew had been a surprise addition to the in-person event. A producer had reached out saying they were interested in doing a documentary on abuse in homeschool communities, but during our initial phone call, I ended up talking about Tears of Eden most of the time. When the producer heard we were having a retreat of sorts for survivors, with people from sixteen states and two countries, she put things in motion to try to send a cameraperson to capture the stories.

I didn't know if they'd be coming until a few weeks before. When they gave me the thumbs-up, saying they'd bought their tickets, I sent out texts and phone calls to the other organizers so we could let attendees know they could opt out of being filmed if they chose. Cult survivors and spiritual abuse survivors sometimes need to maintain their privacy for safety reasons. While safety was my main priority, I knew the presence of a documentary team could potentially bring a layer of validation to the experience.

Survivors often exist in the shadow world, disconnected by trauma from the everyday routine of normal living. We rarely have opportunities to connect with others who understand, carrying our trauma in our bodies and doing our best to pretend everything is fine. While most of us find other survivors through social media, forming pods of community through video calls and chat rooms, we almost never have opportunities to be together in person.

I knew the event was going to be special, but planning it immediately became an impractical endeavor. A thousand times during the year of planning I said, "What am I doing?" Launching a brand-new event is extremely difficult under the best of circumstances, but throughout the year of preparations, I encountered multiple circumstances that activated my own trauma—some of which seemed to come out of nowhere, as triggers sometimes do.

One morning, I woke up with a stress rash that consumed my entire face. *What am I doing?*

As much as I struggled leading up to the date of the event, all of my worries disappeared when I picked up the speaker, Connie Baker, from the airport at 10 p.m. Thursday.

During the fifteen-minute drive from the airport to the guesthouse where Connie would be staying, we laughed twice. We both remarked how easy it was and how perfectly our instant camaraderie fit with the theme of the event, "Laugh Again."

Oh, the sweet relief when you can tap into genuine laughter after the impact of spiritual abuse. I determined that the event would be a success if each participant got a chance to belly laugh at least once over the weekend.

At the happy hour welcome event, attendees began rolling in. Some were folks I'd spoken to over video call or interacted with on social media. Some were genuine strangers who I only recognized by name when they introduced themselves.

The film crew arrived, fitted me with a mic, and began interacting with survivors, asking questions, collecting stories. A half hour or so into the festivities, I realized I'd forgotten the tape for labeling the food and beverages. Since we were hosting the happy hour in one of the common spaces of my apartment complex, I sent Connie and Lily, one of Tears' board members at the time, to my apartment to retrieve the tape.

Once they returned, they immediately approached me, giggling like schoolgirls. Connie said, "As we were rummaging through your drawer, Lily said, 'What if we find sex toys?'"

I chuckled. "Funny enough, that's actually the same drawer I keep my sex toys in. You probably touched them!"

We howled with laughter. Only later did I remember I was wearing a hot mic. I had another laugh about it with the film crew, who'd heard the conversation when they listened back to the recording.

We hosted our speaker session at the zoo, in a room with an aquarium with fish swimming, providing a live sensory calm. Our breakout sessions consisted of yoga, improv, dance, and writing workshops, opportunities to embody our healing—a chance to create and play in the company of folks who understood the long, perilous journey we traveled to arrive at enough safety where we could laugh again.

In one of her talks, Connie shared something I found incredibly helpful for my season of life at the time. She said we have dozens of different life domains—family, friends, hobbies, etc.—and at no one time is everything going to be perfect in every domain. But that doesn't mean we can't thrive. We can live a vibrant life, even if we have a lot of pain and difficulty happening in one or more domains at a time.

Healing. Recovery. Freedom. It doesn't mean a life free of difficulties. But the difficulties do not determine our opportunities and capacity to thrive.

Later, at the farewell breakfast, after my crack-of-dawn interview with the documentary team, I was in the common space conversing with a participant who'd come over from England. She prompted me to turn around. When I did, I saw the remaining attendees gathered around a table, family-style. The morning sun shone through the floor-to-ceiling window and seemed to heighten the atmosphere of warmth coming off that table as the community interacted with one another with wide smiles and the comfort of a thousand conversations—though most of them had just met that weekend.

Tears constricted the back of my throat, and my eyes filled.

It was a snapshot of hope for life on the other side.

ENDNOTES

CHAPTER ONE

3 **Christians would take over the world:** "FOR OUR
DAUGHTERS Official Film," YouTube video, 29:24, posted
by Kristin Kobes Du Mez, September 26, 2024,
youtube/IkES4X_qb6c?si=r_OG0vc0ATMlpL4P.

6 **Alyssa Wakefield married a Welch:** "Groomed for
an Abusive Arranged Marriage: Alyssa Wakefield's
Story PART 1," YouTube video, 1:01:23, posted
by Sheila Wray Gregoire, June 9, 2022. youtu.be/
L30iZuwY4Qk?si=6X7yRBqs8Rp-a3tH.

6 **Christian patriarchy movement:** The leaders of this
movement include Doug Phillips, Doug Wilson, and Bill
Gothard. Less cultic but still fundamentalist and influential
are James Dobson, Jerry Falwell, and C.J. Mahaney.
(Observations mine.)

CHAPTER TWO

25 **God came first, the father second, and the
wife and children fell beneath that:** Tim Chastain,
"Patriarchy, Bill Gothard, and the Umbrella of
Protection," *Jesus Without Baggage*, July 20, 2019,

jesuswithoutbaggage.wordpress.com/2017/03/13/
patriarchy-bill-gothard-and-the-umbrella-of-protection.

CHAPTER THREE

47 **I interviewed Connie Baker:** Connie Baker, interview
by Katherine Spearing, *Uncertain*, podcast audio, "S4: E6—
Power and Control in Spiritual Abuse with Connie Baker (A
Most Loved Episode)," February 21, 2024, www.tearsofeden.
org/podcast/s4e6-power-and-control-in-spiritual-abuse-with-
connie-baker-a-most-loved-episode.

CHAPTER FOUR

62 **I invited my colleague Laura Anderson:** Laura Anderson,
interview by Katherine Spearing, *Uncertain*, podcast audio,
"S4: E19—Second Wave Fundamentalism with Dr. Laura
Anderson," June 27, 2023, www.tearsofeden.org/podcast/
s4-e19-second-wave-fundamentalism-with-dr-laura-anderson.

CHAPTER SIX

85 **A secure attachment to at least one parent is often
enough to help a child grow up securely attached:** Susan
McGarvie, "Attachment Theory, Bowlby's Stages and
Attachment Styles," *Positive Psychology*, November 28, 2024,
positivepsychology.com/attachment-theory.

88 **Our father disliked what he called "unwholesome
speech":** Abusers have been known to create an image of
goodness by zeroing in on specific "sins." Not only do they
claim to refrain from this sin but they are notorious for
reprimanding others when they commit an infraction. It

creates an appearance of goodness they can hide behind. It might also be a form of self-deception, as they use it as proof they are good people and will often put up a vigorous fight to maintain this image. (Observations mine.)

96 **She DARVOed me:** Anna Smith Haghighi, "What to Know About DARVO," *Medical News Today*, February 15, 2024, www.medicalnews today.com/articles/ what-is-darvo#darvo-and-mental-health.

100 ***Burnout:*** Emily Nagoski and Amelia Nagoski, *Burnout: The Secret to Unlocking the Stress Cycle* (Ballantine Books, 2019).

CHAPTER TEN

163 **It is illegal for a member of the clergy to expect sexual consent from a congregant:** "'Is Clergy Sexual Misconduct Illegal?'" Clergy Sexual Misconduct Information and Resources, accessed October 15, 2024 clergysexualmiscon-duct.com/adult-clergy-abuse-law.

164 **They just might say we aren't human enough to own land:** Catherine Allgor, "Coverture: The Word You Probably Don't Know but Should," *National Women's History Museum*, September 4, 2012, www.womenshistory.org/articles /coverture-word-you-probably-dont-know-should.

CHAPTER TWELVE

181 **I learned what a clitoris is:** Kristine Thomason "All You Need to Know About the Clitoris,"

Health, September 27, 2023, www.health.com/
mind-body/10-things-you-never-knew-about-the-clitoris.

190 **The happiest men are married men:** "Marriage and
Men's Health," Harvard Health Publishing, Harvard Medical
School, June 5, 2019, www.health.harvard.edu/mens-health/
marriage-and-mens-health.

190 **The happiest women are single and child-free:** Sian
Cain, "Women Are Happier without Children or a Spouse,
Says Happiness Expert," *The Guardian*, May 25, 2019,
www.theguardian.com/lifeandstyle/2019/may/25/women-
happier-without-children-or-a-spouse-happiness-expert.

CHAPTER FOURTEEN

203 **The creation of these dark creatures that suck the
souls:** *Harry Potter Wiki*, harrypotter.fandom.com/wiki/
Dementor#.

209 **My colleague Laura Anderson says that we
can't "unlearn" things:** Laura Anderson, interview by
Katherine Spearing, *Uncertain*, podcast audio, "S4:
E19—Second Wave Fundamentalism with Dr. Laura
Anderson," June 27, 2023, www.tearsofeden.org/podcast/
s4-e19-second-wave-fundamentalism-with-dr-laura-anderson.

CHAPTER SIXTEEN

228 **Men who were teachers were given ample opportuni-
ties to try and fail and try again:** Katherine Spearing, "As a
Female Preacher I Was Treated Very Differently to My Male
Counterparts—in the End I Left," *Woman Alive*, July 26,

2023, www.womanalive.co.uk/opinion/as-a-female-preacher-i-was-treated-very-differently-to-my-male-counterparts-in-the-end-i-left/16023.article.

CHAPTER SEVENTEEN

236 **Spiritual abuse affects everything:** Connie Baker, interview by Katherine Spearing, *Uncertain*, podcast audio, "S5: E4—Spiritual Abuse Awareness Month: Thriving After Spiritual Abuse—with Connie Baker," January 30, 2024, www.tearsofeden.org/podcast/s5e4-spiritual-abuse-awareness-month-thriving-after-spiritual-abuse-with-connie-baker.

ACKNOWLEDGMENTS

Thanks to David Morris at Lake Drive Books for taking a chance on this weird little book.

Thanks to all my therapists. Thank you for believing me.

Thanks to Heather Gargis, Halley Kim, Julie Scott, and Cait West for your early feedback on this manuscript. Your insight was invaluable.

Thank you to Dr. Maya Angelou. You showed me what words could be.

Thanks to the editorial board at Tears of Eden. You've made me a better writer.

Thanks to Nikki G. and the board of directors at Tears of Eden for your care of this underserved population of spiritual abuse survivors.

Thank you to Dr. Laura Anderson and the staff at the Center for Trauma Resolution and Recovery for your incredible work supporting survivors and creating resources.

Thanks to Cait West for being my partner in walking many streets, eating much food, and exploring haunted places during our very productive annual writing retreats. Where are we going next year?

Thanks to Dr. Mary Martha Abernathy for every traveling adventure.

Thanks to Heather Gargis. You're my favorite witch.

Thanks to Samantha Rawlings. Your compassion and sense of justice give me hope that there is good in the world worth fighting for.

Thanks to the Renegades. Keep fucking the patriarchy. (Interpret that in whatever way is helpful to you.)

Thank you to the coffee shops who kept me caffeinated while writing this book, particularly Century Coffee, Coma, Northwest Coffee, and Quarrelsome.

Thank you to Nana for loving your grandkids.

Thanks to my sisters for reading my earliest stories and believing in me as a writer. Thanks for everything you taught me in our younger years about life and friendship. I would not have survived without you.

Thank you to Jamie Marino. We were born cousins. We became friends.

Thank you to my improv friends and teammates. Thank you for your support of me while I wrote this book. Thanks for making me laugh and reminding me that fun, all by itself, is valuable.

Thank you to each and every one of my clients. You give me hope every day that what was done to us is not the end of our story. We have the pen now.

Thank you to myself. Keep kicking ass.

ABOUT THE AUTHOR

KATHERINE SPEARING is the founder of Tears of Eden, a nonprofit supporting survivors of spiritual abuse and is a Certified Trauma Recovery Practitioner with a Master of Arts in Religion and Cultures. For five seasons, she hosted the groundbreaking podcast *Uncertain*, pioneering pivotal conversations around abuse in churches. In addition to working with survivors of trauma and abuse, she is an author, sought-after podcast guest, and advocate for women reclaiming their autonomy after systemic oppression.

ABOUT LAKE DRIVE BOOKS

Lake Drive Books is an independent publishing company
offering books that help you heal, grow, and discover.
We champion books about values and strategies, not ide-
ologies, and authors who are spiritually rich, contextually
intelligent, and focused on human flourishing.
We want to help readers feel seen.

If you like this or any of our other books at
lakedrivebooks.com, we could use your help:
Please follow our authors on social media, subscribe
to their newsletters, and tell others what you think
of their remarkable books.